LOVE IS NOT BLIND

Discerning Fake Love

by
ANUROOP SEBASTIAN

Published by:
Creative Press
P. O. Box 769000
Dallas, Texas 75376-9000

Volume 1 in The Discerning Series
First Edition

ISBN: 978-0-89985-505-9 (Paperback edition)
ISBN: 978-0-89985-523-3 (Hardcover edition)
ISBN: 978-0-89985-524-0 (eBook edition)

Library of Congress Control Number: 2016937094

Publisher's Cataloging-In-Publication Data
(Prepared by The Donohue Group, Inc.)

Names: Sebastian, Anuroop.
Title: Love is not blind : discerning fake love / by Anuroop Sebastian.
Description: First edition. | Dallas, Texas : Creative Press, [2019] | Series: The
    discerning series ; volume 1 | Includes bibliographical references.
Identifiers: ISBN 9780899855059 (paperback) | ISBN 9780899855233
    (hardcover) | ISBN 9780899855240 (ebook)
Subjects: LCSH: Love--Religious aspects--Christianity. | Discernment (Christian
    theology) | Spiritual warfare. | Love in the Bible.
Classification: LCC BV4639 .S43 2019 (print) | LCC BV4639 (ebook) | DDC
    241.4--dc23

This book is available for purchase in bulk. For orders and inquiries, please contact me.

TABLE OF CONTENTS

ACKNOWLEDGMENTS

I would like to personally thank and dedicate this book to everyone who has helped me to grow in the Lord. Each one of you is a gift from God. You have helped to bear my burdens. Many of you have carried the heavy end of several logs with me. If I have succeeded in great trials as I traveled through dark and dangerous paths, it is because you lent me your torches in the first place. I am grateful.

May God richly bless you with the grace that is needed to fulfill your calling.

INTRODUCTION

DISCERNING FAKE LOVE

Wounds from a friend can be trusted, ***but an enemy multiplies kisses.***

(Proverbs 27:6 NIV)

One day while praying, I saw a vision: In this vision, I saw a close friend of mine, a professing Christian, trying to hang me. At that time, I rarely saw visions; I was shocked by it and didn't understand what it meant. This vision was not a result of my imagination because I would never have imagined that my close friend would attempt to kill me. This was very confusing to me because the person I saw in the vision appeared to be very nice. But I knew that the vision was from God.

Somebody said, "truth is stranger than fiction," meaning that reality can be more bizarre than anything that can be imagined. During the subsequent years, I came to know that this person had a history of psychological illness, which of course I didn't know about when I saw the vision. The miswiring of the certain regions of the brain may cause psychological illnesses. However, that was not the reason for this person's mental condition. The Bible shows that in some cases, these disorders are connected to demons, as seen in the biblical account of the madman of Gadara (Mark 5).

There were some rare occasions when this person I saw in the vision had extreme and dangerous character fluctuations: He could turn into another person and deeply hurt others. However, he did not have *Multiple Personality Disorder*. There were times when his actions proved that he did not have any conscience or natural affections, and he expressed *absolute* selfishness. For the most part, he appeared to be godly and an extremely spiritual person.

If you had met him, you would have never noticed that he had any kind of mental disorder. For 99.9 percent of the time, he was normal. It appeared as though he had a conscience for that part of the time, but for the other 0.01 percent, there was no conscience. I was absolutely shocked when I came to know about his extreme and dangerous character fluctuations. I never expected that someone who appeared to be a deeply spiritual person could have a strong demonic nature. If I had known about it, I would have stayed away.

Now, let us go back to the vision. I knew that God was speaking to me, but I did not understand the full meaning of the vision, and I didn't take it seriously. After a few weeks, I received a phone call from this person I saw in the vision and had a short chat with him over the phone. The next night, tragedy struck—I couldn't sleep! I was shocked. I think I eventually fell asleep around 6 am and woke up after an hour. This was a strange experience for me. Some people suffer from insomnia due to stress, but I was not in any stressful situation that might cause me to lose sleep. This life of sleeplessness later developed into a pattern; from then on, I only slept a few hours every day. Then I remembered the warnings in the vision.

Many of my Christian friends prayed for my deliverance. But I did not get healed, and the insomnia persisted. I was wondering why my prayers were not being answered. Then, I attended a ministers' conference. After I returned from the conference, I slept well.

I also saw a second vision. In this one, I saw the same person from the previous vision, but now he was carrying a gun. He was looking for an opportunity to shoot me. I saw myself barely escaping being killed by him. So I stopped communicating with the person from these visions.

I began to ponder these matters before the Lord. What is the meaning of all these strange experiences? How did I suddenly get insomnia? As I was praying over it, God also began to impress upon my heart to stay away from a few other individuals whom I considered to be friends.

After a lengthy season of prayer, I heard the voice of God. God said, "Do not accept their love!" When I heard the voice of God, I was alone in my apartment. Then, I realized that the love and friendship that were given to me by my so-called friends were fake. **The meaning of the two visions that I mentioned is about spiritual contamination, not physical threats. The man that I saw in the visions does not have a violent nature.**

Most people think that the devil will come in with a red suit and a pitchfork in his hand. Don't be naive! The Bible says, "Satan himself is transformed into an angel of light" (2 Corinthians 11:14, KJV). Jesus said that we need to watch out for false prophets who are ferocious wolves; but they will come in sheep's clothing (Matthew 7:15).

I chose the title of the book, *Love is Not Blind:Discerning Fake Love*, to expose Satan's ability to imitate God's love. The words "fake" and "counterfeit" mean the same thing—a fraudulent imitation of something that is valuable. Satan has a strategy to create counterfeit or fake love, which is not the real thing. You may be sincerely giving true love to your friend. But is your friend paying you back with fake love? Accepting fake love will give you great joy, but it leads to deception. Sure, the devil will generously pay you, but the cash is counterfeit.

This book is about relationships. It gives readers the wisdom to recognize their true friends and enables them to safeguard themselves from toxic relationships.

And lead us not into temptation, but deliver us from the evil one.
(Matthew 6:13 NIV)

Matthew 6:13 commands us to pray for protection from the evil one. May the Lord give us the wisdom to discern fake love. I humbly thank you for reading the first volume of *The Discerning Series*.

Your brother in Christ,
Anuroop Sebastian

Chapter One

Friendship is Accepting a

Person's Love

There are so many definitions of love. I think the best definition is that when you love someone, you place great value on that person. The value that you place on your friends will be evidenced not by what you say to them, but by the way that you treat them. That's what counts.

Friendships

Friendships begin when you accept a person's love. If you do not accept someone's love, you are not his or her friend. I am so glad to have genuine friends in my life. My friends have encouraged, advised, and corrected me many times. Friends are treasures; they are gifts from God. They have given so much to me. When I was going through some of the most difficult times in my life, it was my friends who helped me through it. They came to help me when my whole world was falling apart. I could never repay them, even in a lifetime. To be sure I'm on the right track, I have friends to whom I frequently talk. These individuals are some of the most valuable assets in my life.

Let me start by asking you this question: Do you have such friends— loyal and trustworthy—who value you and show you how much they value you? Many people do not have these kinds of friends. The reason is that at one time in their lives they trusted someone very deeply, only to discover that they had been betrayed. Now, they cannot or will not allow themselves to trust anyone again.

The Power of Agreement

Can two walk together, unless they are agreed?

(Amos 3:3)

Why is it hard to find *covenant friends*? The answer is simple: It is hard to find someone who can fully understand your life's journey. To fully understand someone, it may involve at least one of these three possibilities:

1. It could be because you both have gone through similar life experiences. A true friend understands your pain because he has gone through similar experiences. Even though they are not the exact same experiences, these experiences in life give two individuals a common perspective.
2. Two people have a mutual attraction to each other's personality. In other words, it's the chemistry between two people.
3. It is a friendship that is developed over time, and it becomes a strong bond.

Our covenant friends are intimately interconnected with each other. They will always be on your side to help you meet your destiny, and one of their main goals in life is to see you succeed. True friends rejoice at your success. They are not envious or intimidated by your achievements, because you cannot be envious of people you love. True friends are not seeking to get something from you to promote themselves. They want to give more than to receive. You can share your innermost thoughts with them. I believe that if you have at least two true covenant friends, you are a blessed person. You do not need a lot of friends, but you do need a few good ones.

PAUL'S FRIENDSHIP WITH TIMOTHY

*At my **first defense** no one stood with me, but all forsook me. May it not be charged against them.*

(2 Timothy 4:16)

In 2 Timothy 4:16, Paul is referring to his first trial at the Roman Imperial Court. None of his friends stood by him to testify for his defense during the trial. All of his friends forsook him because associating with Paul was costing them. If betrayal can happen to the apostle Paul, it can also happen to us.

One good example of a covenant friendship is the relationship between the apostle Paul and Timothy. Paul poured his life into Timothy, and Timothy valued Paul. Timothy was on Paul's side in good times and bad times.

ACCEPTING A PERSON'S LOVE

As I mentioned earlier, friendships always begin when you accept a person's love; if you do not accept someone's love, you are not his or her friend. I believe there are three main factors in developing friendships:
1. Accepting a person's love.
2. The level of uniformity of thoughts, opinions, perspectives, and beliefs.
3. The level of uniformity of character traits.

Accepting a person's love is the reason that friendships develop.

Next, there must also be something in common. You are comfortable with others who share your opinions and have similar character traits. Even though best friends may not agree on everything, there has to be a high level of uniformity in fundamental beliefs to establish solid friendships. It is impossible to become best friends when there are too many wide disagreements and major differences of opinions.

Some friends are like "Teflon" nonstick cookware. In the beginning it is very shiny, but after a while, when the pressure of heat is applied, it eventually falls apart. This is the ultimate test of friendship: When everyone else walks away, who will be on your side? Real friends will stick with you at the most trying times in your life, even if supporting you may cost them something in the end. They bear each other's burdens. *Real love will always cost you.* This is the kind of friend I like to be. And these are the kinds of friends I like to have.

CHAPTER TWO

WHO IS YOUR FRONT ROW

AUDIENCE?

T he author of the poem, *Life is a Theater*, compares each of us to an actor performing on the stage. The audience represents the people in our lives. Those who love us have the front row seats, and those in the balcony are the ones you have to love from a distance. The author differentiates between the ones who are among the front row audience and the ones who are sitting in the balcony. We need to be careful of the people we allow to sit in the front row of our lives.

The ones who sit on the front row are important to you because you observe their response while you are performing the act. If they cheer for you, you get the encouragement to perform better. If they do not respond to your performance, it can discourage you. The ones who sit on the front row are the ones with whom you can be totally transparent; you can open your lives to them. You can talk about your weaknesses and fears to them. *You can trust them with your secrets, and they do not share your secrets on Facebook.*

When you share your secrets with others, you are establishing strong relationships. You are telling them that you trust them with your secrets. The more genuine your friendships are, the more transparent you will become to them. However, you must be prepared; there will be very few of them you can totally trust.

Tears and Laughter

There will also be times of tears and laughter. None of us is perfect. All of us can have misunderstandings. Your friends may hurt you, and you may hurt your friends. So, there will be times when you will have to cry with your friends; there will be tears. Then, you will have times when you will laugh together as you get over the hurts that you've caused each other. *All of us have to put up with each other.*

All of it comes down to one major question: Does your friend truly love you, in spite of the fact that he has caused you hurt or pain?

To answer this question, I am putting myself on the spot. There are times when I have lost my temper, and because of it I hurt my friends with my words, even though I loved them. I was wrong. After I had cooled off, I apologized to them. But I sincerely love my friends, and I am willing to pay the price to keep their friendship.

False Friends

I once paid for my groceries with a $100 bill. Immediately, the clerk took the bill and examined it to see if it was real or counterfeit. Like currency, love is very valuable. Fake love is like counterfeit currency. You may sincerely love your friend and are giving pure love from your heart. But is your friend paying you back with counterfeit love?

When you establish friendships, you are also taking a risk because you are establishing a relationship with someone you do not know very well. Knowing someone takes time. When you know more about a person, your love for that person can increase if he is a genuine person. This can also be true in the opposite direction. After I had the opportunity to know more about my *so-called* friends, the less I loved them.

Some *false* friends are very convincing; they are the *convincing counterfeits*. I have made the mistake of establishing friendships with the wrong people. I became very close to them too quickly. As months and years passed by, I noticed that I made a big mistake. I acted foolishly by becoming their friends. By then, it was too late; I had already shared all my personal stories with them. But I have learned from my mistakes. Now, I choose my friends very carefully.

Not everyone can be in your front row. Some people in your life should be in the balcony. I have to be honest with you: There are some people I never want to meet again (including some preachers). I do not hate them; I love them from a distance because they have deeply hurt me. And if I get close to them, they will hurt me again. I thought they loved me, but they were only using me. These people have the nature of the devil. It is their nature to hurt others, just like the nature of the scorpion is to sting its prey. If I see those kinds of people, I run as fast as possible.

Everyone who approaches you does not always have the right intentions. There will always be those who will try to take advantage of you.

DRAINING RELATIONSHIPS

There are also those who fall into the category of *draining* relationships—they drain the life out of you. The devil will cause those draining relationships to come into our lives. We waste so much time with these people that we forget about the genuine relationships. Some people want to become close to you to be *emotionally satisfied*, especially if they are going through stressful situations, which will be most of the time for them. You become their emotional garbage dump. They are parasites who drag your life into their mess. *We can only help people who truly want to change.* Ultimately, they need to seek the help of God to fix their lives.

I recommend that you do an assessment of your life by asking yourself these relationship questions:

1. Do I trust someone whom I do not know very well?
2. Do I share my personal secrets to someone I just met?
3. Do I ignore the signs in someone that show selfishness and a lack of trust?
4. Does these people get close to me *merely* for emotional satisfaction when going through stressful situations? Am I their emotional garbage dump?
5. Since love has value, what is my value in their sight?
6. What is the motivation of someone who wants to become my friend?
7. Finally, here is the most important relationship question: Since only God knows a person's heart, what does God say about your friend?

Rejoice with those who rejoice; mourn with those who mourn.
(Romans 12:15 NIV)

Your true friends celebrate your success; they are not jealous of you. It is such a joy for me to see my friends succeed in life. I am not rejoicing at my friends' success because I expect to personally benefit from it in any way, but I share in their joy. I have to admit that you will find many who will weep with you. But it is hard to find someone who will sincerely rejoice at your success. You need to associate with people who can celebrate you.

CHAPTER THREE

DISCERNMENT IS ANOTHER

LEVEL OF SEEING

Discernment is not a matter of simply telling the difference between right and wrong; rather it is telling the difference between **right** and **almost right**.

—Charles Spurgeon

Discernment is the ability to distinguish between right and what "appears" to be right, but is actually totally wrong. It is a powerful gift from God. We are living in a world that has many voices. Finding the right and true voice is a challenge. In John 10:14–16, Jesus said:

14 I am the good shepherd; and I know My sheep, and am known by My own.

15 As the Father knows Me, even so I know the Father; and I lay down My life for the sheep.

16 And other sheep I have which are not of this fold; them also I must bring, and they will hear My voice; and there will be one flock and one shepherd.

God speaks to us today. However, we need to have the ability to discern the voice of God among the many other voices.

TO LOVE IS TO GIVE VALUE

To love someone means to give great value to that person. The Bible says, "God is love." Love is God's nature. Jesus died on the cross for us because He loves us. We can say that Jesus died on the cross because He has great value for us.

The early Christian writer, Tertullian, said: "The devil is God's monkey." Tertullian was referring to the devil's method of operation: Satan imitates God.

> *And no wonder! For Satan himself transforms himself into an angel of light.*
>
> (2 Corinthians 11:14)

Since God is love, the voice of God is the voice of Love. The devil is a liar and a deceiver. Jesus called Satan "the father of lies and of all that is false" (John 8:44, AMP). The devil hates mankind, and he wants to destroy us through his lies. The devil's main strategy of deception is to imitate God's voice and His nature. This is why it is so important for us to discern the voice of true love from the voice of fake love.

KING SOLOMON'S PRAYER

King David was the second king of Israel, and he lived a life that was pleasing to God. Solomon, the son of David, was chosen by God to become the next king. Solomon knew the enormous task that was ahead of him, and he knew that he was inadequate to lead the nation of Israel. He prayed to God for wisdom.

*9 Therefore give to Your servant an understanding heart to judge Your people, that I may **discern between good and evil**. For who is able to judge this great people of Yours?"*
10 The speech pleased the Lord, that Solomon had asked this thing.

(1 Kings 3:9–10)

Solomon prayed and asked God to give him the ability to discern between good and evil. God was pleased with Solomon's request, so He gave him the supernatural wisdom to discern between good and evil.

Wisdom is seeing things as God sees; it is the ability to know what God's viewpoint is on a matter. Soon, Solomon's wisdom was tested. Two women came to him to solve a difficult problem. They both claimed to be the biological mother of a baby. Obviously, one of them was lying. Solomon had to identify the *real* mother of the baby. We read this story in 1 Kings 3:16–28:

16 Now two women who were harlots came to the king, and stood before him.
17 And one woman said, "O my lord, this woman and I dwell in the same house; and I gave birth while she was in the house.
18 Then it happened, the third day after I had given birth, that this woman also gave birth. And we were together; no one was with us in the house, except the two of us in the house.
19 And this woman's son died in the night, because she lay on him.
20 So she arose in the middle of the night and took my son from my side, while your maidservant slept, and laid him in her bosom, and laid her dead child in my bosom.
21 And when I rose in the morning to nurse my son, there he was, dead. But when I had examined him in the morning, indeed, he

was not my son whom I had borne."

22 Then the other woman said, "No! But the living one is my son, and the dead one is your son." And the first woman said, "No! But the dead one is your son, and the living one is my son." Thus they spoke before the king.

23 And the king said, "The one says, 'This is my son, who lives, and your son is the dead one'; and the other says, 'No! But your son is the dead one, and my son is the living one.'"

24 Then the king said, "Bring me a sword." So they brought a sword before the king.

25 And the king said, "Divide the living child in two, and give half to one, and half to the other."

26 Then the woman whose son was living spoke to the king, for she yearned with compassion for her son; and she said, "O my lord, give her the living child, and by no means kill him!" But the other said, "Let him be neither mine nor yours, but divide him."

27 So the king answered and said, "Give the first woman the living child, and by no means kill him; she is his mother."

28 And all Israel heard of the judgment which the king had rendered; and they feared the king, for they saw that the wisdom of God was in him to administer justice.

REAL MOTHER VS. FAKE MOTHER

In this story, we see the first manifestation of the wisdom of God in the life of Solomon. Solomon wanted to test the hearts of these women, so he gave an order to kill the baby to observe their reactions. He knew that the *real* mother would do anything to protect her baby because mothers have an innate affection for their children.

By giving the order to cut the baby into two pieces, Solomon changed the circumstances surrounding the situation. If the baby were killed, no one would have him. Solomon knew that the *real* mother of the baby could not face her baby being killed. The *real* mother attempted to the save him by allowing the other woman to have the baby, but the other woman (*fake* mother) expressed no sorrow if the baby was cut into pieces. Solomon found the *real* mother by discovering who loved the baby.

Solomon could not look into the hearts of these two women to find out who was speaking the truth. So, he changed the scene with an idea: the order to kill the baby. He put pressure on both women. Under this pressure, the *real* mother quickly tried to save the baby. But the *fake* mother did not have any sorrow and did not even care that the baby was going to be killed. The change in this scenario revealed the truth. What was the first manifestation of the wisdom of God that was seen in the life of Solomon in answer to his prayer? *Solomon was able to discern between fake love and true love.*

Chapter Four

Listen to Hearts,

Instead of Words

Indeed there is a **counterfeit love**, that often appears among those who are led by a spirit of delusion.
—Jonathan Edwards,
Revivalist of the U.S. Great Awakening

I believe that in order to discern the true nature of others, you need to listen to their hearts instead of listening to their words or following their actions. In the life of Jesus, the supernatural ability of discernment had always been in operation. To discern true love, Solomon had to change the scene; he did it by giving the order to kill the baby. Unlike Solomon, Jesus had the ability to look straight into people's hearts and find out if they truly loved Him. Jesus did not have to change the scene or use pressure to discern true love.

Knowing Their Thoughts?

Knowing their thoughts, Jesus said, *"Why do you entertain evil thoughts in your hearts?*

(Matthew 9:4 NIV)

There are machines like the SPECT scan that show activity in the brain. But there is no machine that can read someone's thoughts. Yet Jesus even knew the thoughts of men. When Jesus saw Nathaniel for the first time, He said, "Here truly is an Israelite in whom there is no deceit" (John 1:47, NIV). Jesus looked into Nathaniel's heart and saw that he was a man with pure motives.

In John 6, Jesus performed a great miracle. Jesus fed thousands of people with five barley loaves and two small fish. The loaves and fish were supernaturally multiplied, as it was distributed. Hence, He immediately had a lot of followers. Jesus knew the true intentions of these people. They were following Him because of the free food that was given to them.

As the days passed by, most of these people forsook Jesus. This was no surprise to Him. Jesus knew from the beginning who would leave Him (John 6:64). Most of the crowds who were following Jesus were fickle—they wanted to crown Jesus one day and then crucify Him the next day.

In John 2:24, Jesus rejects the praises of a certain group of people. Their praises appear to be genuine, but Jesus knows that they are simply flattering Him. Yet when Mary pours expensive perfume on His feet, He accepts her love (John 12:1–8). Jesus saw that the act of pouring the ointment was a token of pure love. Jesus rejected the fake love of the people in John 2:24, but He accepted the true love of Mary. *Jesus had the ability to discern the true nature of others by listening to their hearts instead of listening to their words or following their actions.*

In the Gospels, we see that Jesus loved everybody. However, He did not become friends with everyone. Jesus had his friends and the twelve disciples. Jesus loved all his disciples, but out of the twelve disciples, Jesus had three very intimate friends: Peter, James, and John.

Now as he thus made his defense, Festus said with a loud voice, "Paul, you are beside yourself! **Much learning is driving you mad!"**

(Acts 26:24)

When we see what others cannot see, and hear what others cannot hear, we will be misunderstood. Jesus said, "Whoever has ears, let them hear" (Matthew 11:15, NIV). The religious leaders at Jesus' time said that Jesus was insane and demon-possessed. This can happen to us, as well, if we grow in discernment because we are receiving understanding, which most people do not have.

SINCERE LOVE

[Let your] love be sincere (a real thing); *hate what is evil [loathe all ungodliness, turn in horror from wickedness], but hold fast to that which is good.*

(Romans 12:9 AMP)

Are we receiving *sincere* love from others? The word "sincere" came into existence from the Latin phrase "sin cera," which means "without wax." In ancient Greece, pottery was used for the storage of food, oil, and wine. When the pottery was placed in the oven for the clay to harden or dry, some of the pots would develop cracks and were less valuable because they could no longer store liquids. However, unethical potters would fill the cracks with wax, and then cover the wax with paint. Honest potters had to advertise that the pottery was "sin cera," meaning "without wax."

THE HEAT AND PRESSURE TEST

When the pottery was used for cooking and there was wax, it would melt; when heat is applied, the truth is known. In the story of Solomon, Solomon changed the scene by applying pressure—he applied the *heat and pressure test*. Under pressure, the true love of the *real* mother came out, as she tried to save her son by giving him to the *fake* mother.

One way to find out if love is sincere is when the heat and pressure test is applied. The heat and pressure test is not the best way to discern fake love. The best way is when God reveals a person's heart to you. Jesus knew ahead of time who would leave Him.

> *12 Now if anyone builds on this foundation with gold, silver, precious stones, wood, hay, straw,*
> *13 each one's work will become clear; for the Day will declare it, because it will be revealed by fire; and the fire will test each one's work, of what sort it is.*
> *14 If anyone's work which he has built on it endures, he will receive a reward.*
> *15 If anyone's work is burned, he will suffer loss; but he himself will be saved, yet so as through fire.*
>
> (1 Corinthians 3:12–15)

The elements like wood, hay, and stubble could be found in plenty, but gold, silver, and precious stones were hidden and rare. Yet, only the gold, silver, and precious stones endured the test of fire. Everything else will be burned away. When the test of fire is applied, true love will survive and fake love will disappear.

SINCERELY WRONG

None of the disciples of Jesus thought that they would deny Him. All of them except Judas believed that they would even die for Jesus. When

Jesus said that Peter would deny Him three times, Peter said that he would never deny Jesus. Yet, when Jesus was taken captive, all of the disciples ran away in fear for their lives. Peter denied Jesus. Jesus knew them more than they knew themselves. Jesus saw the strengths and weaknesses of his disciples. All of the eleven disciples except Judas were sincere. But, they were sincerely wrong.

FAKE LOVE APPEARS LIKE TRUE LOVE

*And though I bestow all my goods to feed the poor, and though I give my body to be burned, **but have not love, it profits me nothing**.*

(1 Corinthians 13:3)

Giving money to the poor is supposed to be an expression of love. Becoming a martyr for Jesus by allowing oneself to be burned alive is supposed to be an expression of love. One simple observation: we consider people who have sacrificed so much as our role models. But why did they suffer so much? Were all their sufferings birthed out of their love for others and their love for Jesus? Only God knows the true intentions of a person's heart. Let us not judge people by their outward actions alone; we need to look into their hearts to know their true intentions.

For this is the love of God, that we keep His commandments. And His commandments are not burdensome.

(1 John 5:3)

If we say that we love God and do not obey God, it is not scriptural love. It's a fake love—a substitute for the real thing. In the contemporary charismatic movement, we have lost the reverence for God. Some

Christians have a "buddy-buddy" attitude in their relationship with Jesus. It is true that we need to be comfortable in coming to Jesus. However, Jesus is more than your casual friend. We should never lose that sense of awe.

DISCERNMENT—THE MARK OF SPIRITUAL MATURITY

*Solid food is for those who are **mature**, who through training have the skill to recognize the **difference between right and wrong**.*

(Hebrews 5:14 NLT)

*But solid food belongs to those **who are of full age**, that is, those who by reason of use have their senses exercised to **discern both good and evil**.*

(Hebrews 5:14)

Godly discernment is the identifying mark of spiritual maturity. Spiritual maturity produces discernment. Hence, discerning between true love and fake love can only be accomplished if we walk closely with God. Jesus discerned even the thoughts of men. If we walk with Jesus, He will reveal even the thoughts of the ones who approach us. You need to live with your *spiritual antenna* raised towards Heaven.

The Bible teaches us that the greatest commandment is to love the Lord with all our hearts and to love our neighbor as ourselves (Matthew 22:36–40). We should obey the commandment of love. At the same time, we should also have the ability to discern if the love that we get from others is true or counterfeit.

At one point in my life, there were a few people whom I considered to be close friends. But later on, I discovered that I had greatly misjudged some of these people. Some of them were wolves in sheep's clothing. The Church is supposed to be a safe place, but there are a lot of religious insincerities, backstabbing, and hypocrisy in our churches today.

I pray that this book will help you cultivate this gift of discernment. As you read through the book, you will learn to discern the true nature of others by listening to their hearts, instead of going by your natural feelings.

CHAPTER FIVE

BRAIN VS. MIND

The materialists believe that physical matter is the only reality in the universe, and everything that happens in this world is subjected to physical processes, or even reduced to matter. In this view, the human mind, thoughts, and emotions are the result of chemical processes that happen in the brain. Therefore, the materialists believe that our consciousness, personality, and perception are simply an output of a biological machine called the brain.

This perspective has a profound influence on how the materialists propose to treat mental disorders or therapy. Imagine being treated for depression by someone who views your personality and identity as a machine output in need of mechanical fine-tuning. According to the chemical imbalance theory of depression, depression is the result of having too much or too little of certain brain chemicals, and antidepressants correct this imbalance. However, a report from Harvard Medical School states that depression is not merely the result of a chemical imbalance in the brain; depression is a complex disease that has many possible causes.[1] A purely mechanical, materialist view doesn't capture the complexity of who we are.

MIND OVER MATTER

If the thoughts and behavior are purely the result of brain activity, then criminal activities have to be excused. After all, based on the *materialist's* point of view, the brain of a criminal is actually producing the thoughts to commit crimes.

Many neuroscientists believe that the mind controls the brain; this means that the mind is completely different from the brain. Our thoughts have the power to change the brain. In fact, negative thinking can damage the neural structures of the brain. New research indicates that having a high sense of purpose in life reduces the probability of having a stroke.[2]

Recent research proves that we have the ability to generate new brain cells. The ability of the brain to change and to adapt through mental activity is known as neuroplasticity.

THOUGHT VS. EMOTION

Thoughts and emotions are intimately connected, and we feel our thoughts. In Chapter 3 ("Discernment is Another Level of Seeing"), we looked into the story where the real mother tried to protect her baby. Based on the fact of being the real mother, she was emotionally attached to her baby. The emotional component is the love that she had for her baby. She protected her baby by allowing the other woman to keep her baby. But not all mothers love their biological children. There are parents/mothers who sell their daughters into the sex trade.

Here is a relevant question that applies to American society: Why do we have so many children in foster care in the U.S.? Where are the biological parents of these children? Why do some parents lack the love-based emotions toward their children? In Chapter 15 ("When Love Disappears"), I briefly share the real reason for the absence of love.

CHAPTER SIX

THE TOTAL MAN

W hat is this emotion that attaches parents to their children? We have named it as love. But what is love? How much love can you give to a person? Where are the boundaries of love? To understand love, we need to study how our body operates from both a spiritual standpoint and a psychological standpoint. There is so much depth to love. To totally understand love, you must see the spiritual aspects of love. Love is more than an emotion. From this chapter onwards, we are going to carefully study the many facets of love, which involve both spiritual and psychological aspects.

Our physical attributes including the color of hair and height are defined in the DNA. The Bible says that God is a Spirit (John 4:24). Man was created in the likeness and in the image of God (Genesis 1:26–27). This means that man is also a spirit being. Just like we get our DNA through our parents, when a person becomes *born again*, he receives the DNA of God. So, what do I mean by being born again? Please read below as I explain.

MAN: AN ETERNAL SPIRIT

*Now may the God of peace Himself sanctify you completely; and may your whole **spirit, soul, and body** be preserved blameless* *at the coming of our Lord Jesus Christ.*

(1 Thessalonians 5:23)

Man is an eternal spirit, and he has a three-fold nature. Man is a spirit; he has a soul, and he lives in a physical body (1 Thessalonians 5:23). As I mentioned in the previous chapter, the mind is separate from the brain. The mind influences the brain. The soul is the mind and the intellect, the part of mankind that reasons and thinks. The brain is the physical organ through which the soul of a person operates in this world.

The Book of Genesis records the creation of mankind. God first made man (Adam) and gave him dominion over all the earth. Man was created in the likeness and in the image of God. He walked and talked with God. He was in perfect fellowship with God. Adam was filled with the love of God that was imparted into his life at creation. But Adam was not equal to God. God said that Adam would die *the day* he ate the fruit (Genesis 2:17). But when he ate the fruit, he did not die physically for more than 900 years. When he disobeyed God, he died spiritually. When Adam sinned, his entire being (spirit, soul, and body) became corrupted. Adam could no longer have the same fellowship with God.

When he sinned, he didn't stop existing as a spirit being. However, the nature of the devil came into his spirit. The spirit of Adam changed into something that is evil. The Divine love that was in Adam was lost. In other words, when sin entered into the life of Adam, he turned into another kind of spirit being—he became a slave of the devil. But Adam still maintained a small portion of the love and affection that he had originally been given. It is the spirit part of the man that brings out the love-based emotions. We are wired by God to walk in love. We are created by God to function in love. Even though Adam's spirit was contaminated, his spirit still maintained a small measure of the love he had once received.

WHO IS TO BLAME?

*Then the man said, "The woman whom You gave to be with me,
she gave me of the tree, and I ate."*

(Genesis 3:12)

When Adam sinned, he cast the blame on Eve. But, Adam was equally
responsible for the sin. Why didn't he acknowledge his sin? Why
did he blame Eve for it? Because he no longer had the Divine love
that he once had for his wife. Instead of protecting Eve by accepting
the responsibility, he blamed Eve for the sin. We can clearly see that
Adam changed into a selfish person, after he sinned. Adam's spirit was
contaminated as he received the nature of the devil.

THE CURSE

*Therefore, just as through one man sin entered the world, and
death through sin, and thus **death spread to all men**, because
all sinned —*

(Romans 5:12)

As Adam sinned, all the descendants of Adam became slaves of the
devil. A man cannot save himself by works, as he has become a slave of
the devil. Romans 5:12 is not talking about physical death, even though
physical death is a part of the curse. Instead, the death that is mentioned
here is spiritual death. Spiritual death means separation from God.

BEING BORN AGAIN

*3 Jesus answered and said to him, "Most assuredly, I say to you,
unless one is born again, he cannot see the kingdom of God."*

4 Nicodemus said to Him, "How can a man be born when he is old? Can he enter a second time into his mother's womb and be born?"
5 Jesus answered, "Most assuredly, I say to you, unless one is born of water and the Spirit, he cannot enter the kingdom of God.
*6 That which is **born of the flesh is flesh, and that which is born of the Spirit is spirit**.*

(John 3:3–6)

Jesus was telling Nicodemus about being born again. Nicodemus was confused about what Jesus said. He asked Jesus about how he could be born a second time. Jesus corrected him and said, "which is born of the Spirit is spirit." Jesus was talking about the rebirth of the spirit of a man.

*For the **wages** of sin is death, but the gift of God is eternal life in Christ Jesus our Lord.*

(Romans 6:23)

Wages are what we earn for the services that are performed. As the result of sin, human beings experienced spiritual death and became the slaves of the devil. God reached out to us when we were under the bondage of Satan. To save mankind, Jesus volunteered Himself to take the punishment for our sins—this is the Divine exchange! The Bible clearly teaches the full deity and the full humanity of Christ. God offers eternal life to us through the price that Jesus paid on the cross. Receiving this life of God through the new birth changes the spiritual nature of man, and we become a new person. We become born again and have the life of Christ in us.

1 Corinthians 13:5 says that God's love is not selfish; it does not

seek its own benefit. The death of Jesus on the cross is the greatest expression of love. Jesus died for us when we were yet sinners. *No one loves us more than Jesus.*

> *Therefore if any man be in Christ, he is a **new creature**: old things are passed away; behold, all things are become new.*
>
> (2 Corinthians 5:17 KJV)

As a person becomes born again, he becomes a new creature. The **new creature** that is referred to here is the spirit of an individual. Now, the spirit of a person has become pure and holy. Old things have not passed away on the outside—that is in his physical body. He will still have the same body he always had. However, he is a *new* person on the inside, and he must let the Holy Spirit guide him. When we are saved, we are born into His family as spiritual babies; we are passed from *spiritual* death to eternal life (1 John 3:14).

Even though the physical body of someone dies, his spirit lives forever. In the story of Lazarus and the rich man, we see the eternal life of the spirit of a man after physical death (Luke 16:19–31). The spirit of man is eternal and can never die.

The apostle Paul said:

23 For I am hard-pressed between the two, having a desire to depart and be with Christ, which is far better.
24 Nevertheless to remain in the flesh is more needful for you.
(Philippians 1:23–24)

When Paul said, "having a desire to depart," he is talking about physical death. The "I" that Paul mentions is his spirit. He wanted to die physically and be with Jesus. The part of his being that will be with Jesus was the real Paul—his spirit.

THE HOLY SPIRIT INSIDE THE HUMAN SPIRIT

Right before Jesus was going to be crucified, He met with his disciples for the Last Supper (John 13).

> *He is the Holy Spirit, who leads into all truth. The world cannot receive him, because it isn't looking for him and doesn't recognize him. But you know him, because **he lives with you now and later will be in you**.*
>
> (John 14:17 NLT)

Since Jesus said, "he lives with you," we understand that the Holy Spirit was with the disciples at the moment Jesus was speaking to them. When Jesus said, "later will be in you," He was looking into the future. He saw the Holy Spirit being inside the believer at the time of the new birth.

> *You are of God, little children, and have overcome them, because He who is in you is greater than he who is in the world.*
>
> (1 John 4:4)

> *And what agreement hath the temple of God with idols? **for ye are the temple of the living God**; as God hath said, I will dwell in them, and walk in them; and I will be their God, and they shall be my people.*
>
> (2 Corinthians 6:16 KJV)

At the new birth, we are born of God. But it doesn't just stop there. The Holy Spirit—the third Person of the Trinity—lives inside a born-again believer. Yes, our human spirits have the capacity of having God living inside us. The Greater One is God Himself, Who lives in our human spirit as the result of the rebirth. This may be too difficult for our minds to understand; if you are born again, the same Holy Spirit Who raised Jesus from the dead lives inside your human spirit.

Romans 10:9 says,

that if you confess with your mouth the Lord Jesus and believe in your heart that God has raised Him from the dead, you will be saved.

Repenting before God, believing and confessing that Jesus died for our sins and was raised from the dead is the point when we have salvation.

THE DNA OF GOD

*Put on your **new nature**, created to be like God — truly righteous and holy.*

(Ephesians 4:24 NLT)

*Through these he has given us his very great and precious promises, so that through them you may **participate in the divine nature**, having escaped the corruption in the world caused by evil desires.*

(2 Peter 1:4 NIV)

When a person becomes born again, he truly becomes a new person. He receives a new nature, which is the nature of God; he receives God's DNA. But the nature of God needs to be developed through spiritual growth. Just like the physical traits of babies are developed as they physically grow, as Christians grow spiritually they develop into the nature of God.

The Spirit of Man–Heart

*A merry **heart** does good, like medicine,*
*But a broken **spirit** dries the bones.*

(Proverbs 17:22)

In Proverbs 17:22, the words, "heart" and "spirit" are used interchangeably. But in other passages, the words, "heart" and "soul" are used interchangeably. The *Oxford Dictionary* defines heart as "the central or innermost part of something."[3] The human spirit is the center of man's being.

3 Do not let your adornment be merely outward — arranging the hair, wearing gold, or putting on fine apparel —
*4 rather let it be the **hidden person of the heart**, with the incorruptible beauty of a **gentle and quiet spirit**, which is very precious in the sight of God.*

(1 Peter 3:3–4)

This passage is referring to the development of the born-again human spirit. The born-again human spirit needs to be developed into a **gentle and quiet spirit**. *The spirit of the person is also referred to as the hidden person of the heart.* Here is another reference to the words, "heart" and "spirit" being used interchangeably.

First, the human spirit is referred to as the person of the heart. This person is as real as the outward man (physical body). *But he is a person of the heart or a person of the spirit.* Second, he is a *hidden person*; this means that he is hidden to the physical senses. You can't see the human spirit with your physical eyes.

HUMAN SPIRIT VS. HUMAN SOUL

*For the word of God is alive and powerful. It is sharper than the sharpest two-edged sword, cutting between **soul and spirit**, between **joint and marrow**. It exposes our innermost thoughts and desires.*

(Hebrews 4:12 NLT)

In this passage, the soul and the spirit are compared to joint and marrow. The human spirit and human soul are closely connected, but they are not the same. The soul is the mind and intellect—the part of man that reasons and thinks. *The brain is the physical organ through which the soul of a person operates in this world.* The brain responds to the mind. So what is man? *Man is a spirit who has a soul and lives in a body. The human soul is a part of the human spirit.*

The biblical reference to the word "heart" has a double application. It can be a reference to the human spirit or the human soul. Most of the time, the heart is a reference to the human spirit. But in some passages, it refers to the human soul. Based on the context of the passage, we can determine which one is meant.

As discussed earlier, in 1 Peter 3:3–4, Peter refers to the human spirit as the "hidden person of the heart." In John 14:27, Jesus said, "Let not your heart be troubled, neither let it be afraid." Here, Jesus is telling the disciples not to be afraid. Jesus' reference to the heart is to the minds of the disciples, which is the human soul.

22 So it was that the beggar died, and was carried by the angels to Abraham's bosom. The rich man also died and was buried. 23 And being in torments in Hades, he lifted up his eyes and saw Abraham afar off, and Lazarus in his bosom.

*24 "Then he cried and said, 'Father Abraham, have mercy on
me, and send Lazarus that he may dip the tip of his finger in
water and cool my tongue; for I am tormented in this flame.'
25 But Abraham said, 'Son, **remember** that in your lifetime you
received your good things, and likewise Lazarus evil
things; but now he is comforted and you are tormented.*

(Luke 16:22–25)

In the story of the rich man and Lazarus, both of them died. The
rich man went to hell, and Lazarus went to Paradise. The rich man
remembered the details of his past life on earth. Even after the body has
disintegrated, the memories and the intellect are not lost. *The physical
body expresses through feelings; the soul expresses through reasoning,
and the human spirit expresses through the conscience.* In Chapter 15
("When Love Disappears"), I will talk about the conscience.

SALVATION OF THE SOUL VS. NEW BIRTH

*Therefore **lay aside** all filthiness and overflow of wickedness,
and receive with meekness **the implanted word**, which is able
to **save your souls**.*

(James 1:21)

James wrote this letter above to Christians. We have to *lay aside* our
sinful nature. The word "save" is taken from the Greek word *sozo*, which
conveys four ideas: salvation, healing, deliverance, and wholeness.

When a person becomes born again, his spirit is reborn; the human
spirit is re-created. But the soul is not fully saved. The salvation of
the soul is a continuous process. *The process of saving the soul is the
process of sanctification.*

The working of the *implanted Word* in our lives saves our souls.

In Philippians 2:12, the apostle Paul told Christians to "work out your own salvation."

When we became born again, we were delivered from the *penalty* of sin. Subsequently, in an ongoing way, we are being delivered from the *power* of sin.

> *1 And you He made alive, who **were dead in trespasses and sins**,*
> *2 in which you **once walked according to the course of this world, according to the prince of the power of the air**, the spirit who now works in the sons of disobedience,*
> *3 among whom also we **all once conducted ourselves in the lusts of our flesh**, fulfilling the desires of the flesh and of the mind, and **were by nature children of wrath**, just as the others.*
> (Ephesians 2:1–3)

In this passage, Paul is talking about the life of a Christian before coming to Christ. An unbeliever is not physically dead—he is [spiritually] dead in trespasses and sins. This passage shows the picture of the entire human race which is in rebellion against God. Because of the rebellion, the whole human race became *dead in trespasses and sins*. As the result of spiritual death, rebellion became a part of our nature. *When sin entered the human race, the spirit died, the soul became a rebel, and the body became corrupted.* The body is now subject to sickness, aging and ultimately death. Through repentance, we are reconciled to God.

CHAPTER SEVEN

DISCERNMENT THROUGH THE

LEADINGS OF THE

HOLY SPIRIT

By a new power of discernment I could see his soul, understand
his inner life and motives.[4]

—John G. Lake (1870–1935)

*7 Because the **carnal mind is enmity against God**; for it is not
subject to the law of God, nor indeed can be.*
*14 For as many as are led by the Spirit of God, these are sons
of God.*

(Romans 8:7,14)

A carnal Christian is governed by his *carnal* mind. A Christian who
is governed by his carnal mind makes decisions based on the five senses
(taste, smell, vision, hearing, and touch). A carnal Christian assesses
others on how he feels. The Spirit of God leads a *mature* Christian;
he assesses others based on the wisdom of God. We need to have the

discernment from the Holy Spirit to choose the right friends.

SEEK DISCERNMENT

3 Yes, if you cry out for discernment,
And lift up your voice for understanding,
4 If you seek her as silver,
And search for her as for hidden treasures;

(Proverbs 2:3–4)

Being led by the Spirit of God is the key to developing discernment. Jesus did not judge people based on their outward actions. He was able to discern the true nature of the people who approached Him. As we walk with God, He will reveal the intentions of those who are around us. Do the people who come near us have selfish agendas? Are they wolves in sheep's clothing? Only God knows the true intentions of an individual. This is why we have to be in constant communion with God so that He can reveal the true nature of others to us. We need to learn to let the Holy Spirit lead us. There are many ways that God leads us today, and we will study them in this chapter. The Holy Spirit leads us through the following ways:

1. The Bible
2. The Inward Witness
3. The Voice of the Holy Spirit
4. Peace of God
5. Visions and Dreams
6. Divine Thoughts
7. Gifts of the Holy Spirit
8. The Gift of Prophecy

THE BIBLE

16 All Scripture is given by inspiration of God, and is profitable for doctrine, for reproof, for correction, for instruction in righteousness,
17 that the man of God may be complete, thoroughly equipped for every good work.

(2 Timothy 3:16–17)

The apostle Paul is instructing Timothy to study the Scriptures. The primary way that God leads a Christian is through the Bible. Developing discernment requires a balanced understanding of the Scriptures. Having a sound understanding of the doctrine of the Bible is the foundation of discernment. The Church needs to follow the teachings of the New Testament. However, keep in mind that the New Testament was written 2,000 years ago in the Greek language. We need to study the historical and cultural context to correctly interpret the Scriptures. We also need to look at the immediate context and the broader context and how it relates to other biblical passages.

What is the Correct Interpretation?

In Luke 6:29 Jesus said,
To him who strikes you on the one cheek, offer the other also. And from him who takes away your cloak, do not withhold your tunic either.

Does this mean that we cannot defend ourselves or call the police when someone attacks us? What is the real meaning of Luke 6:29? This is a teaching on forgiveness. Jesus was saying that when someone hurts us, we should not keep unforgiveness in our hearts.

In 2 Corinthians 13:12, Paul says, "Greet one another with a holy kiss." Is Paul instructing us to kiss each other in church? In Paul's time, it was a cultural tradition to kiss one another as a way of expressing greetings. In our days, it can be compared to shaking hands. In Matthew 5:29, Jesus said,

If your right eye causes you to sin, pluck it out and cast it from you; for it is more profitable for you that one of your members perish, than for your whole body to be cast into hell.

Does this mean we need to amputate our bodies to avoid committing sins? Of course not! Jesus meant that sin is dangerous, and it can destroy your life. We need to know the real meaning of the passages of the Bible. I got saved at the age of ten. As years passed, I understood that I had the wrong interpretation of various biblical passages.

The Bible is God Speaking to You

The Holy Spirit leads us through the Scriptures. He opens our spiritual eyes to see the truths of the Bible (Matthew 11:25). It is true that the canon (list of books considered to be authoritative Scripture) is closed, and the Scripture is complete. However, God can still give us specific instructions about our personal lives that are not explicitly stated in the Bible.

I used to work as an accountant, but then God spoke to me and told me He had called me to be a preacher. There is nowhere in the Bible where it says that I, Anuroop, should leave my job on a certain day to step into full-time ministry. Once I quit my accounting job, I had to choose a Bible college. There are also plenty of Bible colleges. So which one do I choose? God spoke to me to go to Christ for the Nations Institute.

All the twelve early disciples of Jesus left their profession to follow

Him. I did not contradict the teachings of the Bible. I do not recommend that anybody leave their career and go into full-time ministry unless God clearly speaks to do so. If you are a Christian, the Holy Spirit is in you. Jesus said that the Holy Spirit will guide you into all truth.

THE INWARD WITNESS

*The Spirit Himself **bears witness with our spirit** that we are children of God,*

(Romans 8:16)

*But the **Holy Spirit also witnesses to us**; for after He had said before,*

(Hebrews 10:15)

The primary way that God leads a Christian is through the Bible. God also leads us through our **inward witness**. A witness is the one who affirms what is seen, heard or known. Today, in the legal field, we say *eyewitness*. As I explained in the previous chapter, when a person gets born again, the Holy Spirit lives in his spirit. As a born-again believer, there is Someone Else (Holy Spirit) living inside him besides himself. Since the Holy Spirit lives in the spirit of a born-again believer, God communicates to a Christian through his human spirit.

*The Spirit Himself **bears witness with our spirit** that we are children of God,*

(Romans 8:16)

The Holy Spirit **bears witness with our spirit**—the Holy Spirit can affirm the truth in our spirits. This witnessing of the Holy Spirit is called the inward witness. Romans 8:16 does *not* say that the Holy

Spirit is bearing witness with our *mind*. As I described in the previous chapter, our mind is not our spirit; the mind represents the soul. Instead, the Holy Spirit is bearing witness with the human spirit of a born-again believer. So the inward witness is not a mental experience. It is not a voice. *It is an inward intuition or a strong inward knowing from the Holy Spirit. It is a spiritual knowing from God.* The inward witness means that the Holy Spirit is giving the witness to you through your spirit.

> For **it seemed good to the Holy Spirit, and to us**, *to lay upon you no greater burden than these necessary things:*
>
> (Acts 15:28)

Acts 15:28 says that the apostles made decisions, as it "seemed good to the Holy Spirit." What is the meaning of the phrase "seemed good?" The apostles were not making mental decisions. As they waited on God in prayer, God confirmed the answer to their human spirit. The inward witness is a *knowing* in our spirit. Yet it is beyond and more real than mental agreement.

The inward witness is an inward intuition or a strong inward knowing from the Holy Spirit. It is a spiritual knowing from God. Spiritual experiences are hard to explain. We have to experience them to understand them.

> **It seemed good** *and desirable to me, [and so I have determined] also after having searched out diligently and followed all things closely and traced accurately the course from the highest to the minutest detail from the very first, to write an orderly account for you, most excellent Theophilus,*
>
> (Luke 1:3 AMP)

Luke said that he wrote the book of Luke because "it seemed good." When Luke said, "It seemed good," he was referring to the inward witness. Surely, there is nothing more important than writing the Scriptures. Luke could not make a single mistake in the authorship of a book of the Bible.

THE VOICE OF THE HOLY SPIRIT

*While Peter thought about the vision, **the Spirit said** to him, "Behold, three men are seeking you.*

(Acts 10:19)

There were rare occasions when I heard the voice of the Holy Spirit. This is considered a *spectacular* experience. I mention one such experience in Chapter 20 ("Don't Accept Their Love!"). When I heard the voice of the Holy Spirit, it was not audible. Yet, I could hear it as clearly as if it had been audible. I heard it from within me. But just because you heard a voice does not mean that it was the voice of God; there are people in mental asylums because they hear "voices."

THE PEACE OF GOD

And let the peace (soul harmony which comes) from Christ rule (act as umpire continually) in your hearts *[deciding and settling with finality all questions that arise in your minds, in that peaceful state] to which as [members of Christ's] one body you were also called [to live]. And be thankful (appreciative), [giving praise to God always].*

(Colossians 3:15 AMP)

*and the **peace of God, which surpasses all understanding,** will* *guard your hearts and minds through Christ Jesus.*

(Philippians 4:7)

In any sport, the *umpire* or *referee* is the official who enforces the rules and makes the judgment calls of the game. Colossians 3:15 says that the peace of God acts as the umpire. The Holy Spirit manifests Himself by giving us peace, as we are living in His will. The *sure sign* that you are not in the will of God is the lack of peace. If you have faith in God, you have the confidence that God is guiding you. When you trust God, you can have peace even in difficult circumstances. The peace of God **surpasses all understanding**—this supernatural peace of God is above all *natural* understanding or reasoning.

VISIONS AND DREAMS

*And it shall come to pass in the last days, saith God, I will pour out of my Spirit upon all flesh: and your sons and your daughters shall prophesy, **and your young men shall see visions, and your old men shall dream dreams**:*

(Acts 2:17 KJV)

The Bible gives numerous occurrences of how God communicated to people through visions and dreams. The Book of Revelation, the final book of the New Testament, contains an account of John's visions that he received on the Isle of Patmos.

False Visions and False Dreams

And no wonder! For Satan himself transforms himself into an angel of light.

(2 Corinthians 11:14)

I must warn you that you have to be very careful about visions and dreams. Some visions can be hallucinations or a product of our *overactive imaginations* rather than the Spirit of God.

Sometimes, Satan himself brings false visions and false dreams to trick us. *The apostle Paul warns us that Satan can also come in the form of an angel to trick us, meaning that we can see a vision that is from the demonic realm* (2 Corinthians 11:14). Satan is the god of this world, and he can operate in this world.

The False Dream

Once, I was going through a time when I had an important decision to make. Even though I did a lot of research and consulted with others, I could not get the right answer. I was confused about the direction that I needed to go regarding this particular situation. I began to pray to get guidance. I prayed and prayed about it, but I could not get the answer. To my amazement, I had a dream while I was sleeping. In this dream, I saw the answer to this important decision—I was excited! Very soon, I came to know that this dream was totally contrary to God's plan for my life. At the time when I saw the dream, it seemed like God was speaking to me. As I prayed about it, I came to know that Satan was trying to deceive me through this false dream. However, I had many other dreams that were confirmations of what God had already spoken to me.

Divine Thoughts

Since the Holy Spirit lives in you, He can put thoughts in your mind. At the same time, the devil can also put thoughts in your mind. Spiritual warfare always begins in the mind of the believer.

Gifts of the Holy Spirit

In 1 Corinthians 14, the apostle Paul gives instructions about the operation of the gifts of the Holy Spirit. The gift of prophecy, word of knowledge, word of wisdom, and discerning of spirits are among the nine gifts of the Holy Spirit. These spiritual gifts can enable us to develop discernment and also give direction to our lives.

The Gift of Prophecy

Can True Prophets Give False Prophecies?

Some conclude that the proof of a true prophet is 100 percent accuracy in prophetic predictions (Deuteronomy 18:20–22; Jeremiah 23:16–32). In the Old Testament, the prophets had 100 percent accuracy. Even the backslidden prophet Balaam had 100 percent accuracy (Numbers 22–23). In 2 Peter 2:16, the apostle Peter refers to Balaam as the "madness of the prophet."

The *New Testament gift of prophecy* can be divided into two categories: first, the infallible and authoritative words given by Jesus and the biblical authors; second, the New Testament gift of prophecy that has divine authority mixed with human errors.

> *Let two or three prophets speak, and let the **others judge**.*
> (1 Corinthians 14:29)

There are five main spiritual offices in the Church, and they are apostles, prophets, evangelists, pastors, and teachers (Ephesians 4:8–12). The apostle Paul is advising the Corinthian believers to judge the prophecies that came from the prophets (1 Corinthians 14:29). These prophets were members of the church in Corinth. *Notice that Paul addresses them as prophets; if Paul refers to someone as a prophet, he is a true prophet.* Some have debated that Paul was telling the church to judge whether or not the prophets were from God or Satan—I strongly disagree with that assumption. If Paul really meant to test if the prophets were truly from God, he would have said it differently—Paul could have said, "There are some false prophets in your church; so you judge and discover the false prophets." But Paul believed that they were true prophets and referred to them that way.

Even prophecies that come from a true prophet of God must be judged. A true prophet will allow others to judge his prophecies. A New Testament believer, who stands in the office of a prophet, is as human as everyone else. Prophets can misjudge and misunderstand the leading of the Holy Spirit, just like other Christians.

Is a False Prophecy Given to the Apostle Paul?

*And finding disciples, we tarried there seven days: who **said to Paul through the Spirit, that he should not go up to Jerusalem**.*
(Acts 21:4 KJV)

*And having looked up the disciples there, we remained with them for seven days. **Prompted by the [Holy] Spirit, they kept telling Paul not to set foot in Jerusalem**.*
(Acts 21:4 AMP)

The King James Version says that the disciples said, "through the Holy Spirit." The Amplified Version makes it very clear—the disciples were "prompted by the Holy Spirit." Here is what actually happened. The disciples sensed a great danger in Paul's journey to Jerusalem. They used their own interpretation and told Paul not to go to Jerusalem. Yet Jesus had already said that Paul would go through much suffering (Acts

9:16). Paul went to Jerusalem and fulfilled God's plan for his life (Acts 23:11).

From this passage, we learn that the disciples gave the wrong interpretation of what they sensed from God, and they gave a false prophecy. *The disciples gave a false prophecy to the apostle Paul!*

The Prophet's Role

> ***For you can all prophesy one by one***, *that all may learn and all may be encouraged.*
>
> (1 Corinthians 14:31)

In the Old Testament, the prophet spoke and the whole nation had to comply. In the New Testament, there is a change in the role and the function of a prophet. All New Testament believers have the Holy Spirit—every New Testament believer can prophesy (Acts 2:17; 1 Corinthians 14:31). However, that doesn't mean that all believers hold the office of a prophet (Ephesians 4:11).

Testing Prophecies vs. Testing Prophets

> *Let two or three prophets speak, and let the **others judge**.*
>
> (1 Corinthians 14:29)
>
> *19 Do not quench the Spirit.*
> *20 **Despise not prophesying**.*
> *21 **Test all things**; hold fast what is good.*
>
> (1 Thessalonians 5:19–21)

In 1 Thessalonians 5:21, Paul tells us to test all things. The word "test" was used to refer to that of testing the genuineness of metals. Now, look at the context. Paul is saying not to despise prophecies. If prophecies could never go wrong, there is no reason to test them. If you completely despise prophecies due to the possibility of an error, you are quenching the works of the Holy Spirit (1 Thessalonians 5:19). Now, let us look into 1 Corinthians 14:29. Paul is telling the Corinthian believers to judge the prophecies of the prophets who were in their church. Notice, Paul calls them prophets. This means that Paul believed that they were true prophets.

1 Corinthians 14:29 and 1 Thessalonians 5:19–21 present the same message. We need to test the prophecies that come from true prophets. It is entirely possible for New Testament prophets to give accurate prophecies at times and false prophesies at other times. *Then again, in some cases, there may be prophecies with divine authority that are mixed with human error* (cf. prophecies that were given to Paul by the disciples).

> *Beloved, do not believe every spirit, but **test the spirits**, whether they are of God; because **many false prophets** have gone out into the world.*
>
> (1 John 4:1)

Prophets speak on God's behalf from the impulse of a sudden illumination of the Holy Spirit. In the above passage, the apostle John is telling people to test those who have the supernatural ability to prophesy because there are many false prophets. We should test them because Satan's servants can also give accurate prophecies through the power of divination.

1 Thessalonians 5:19–21 says to test the prophecies, while 1 John 4:1 says to test the persons. 1 Thessalonians 5:19–21 says to test the prophetic words because John says, "test all things"—notice the word "things." Such prophecies do not have Scripture-quality authority.

Biblical Prophecies vs. Today's Prophecies

And the words of the LORD are flawless, like silver purified in a crucible, like gold refined seven times.

(Psalm 12:6 NIV)

There is a vast difference between the prophecies in the Bible and the prophecies that are given today. The prophecies in the Bible are already tested. Even though human vessels wrote the Bible, the fire of the Holy Spirit purified the biblical prophecies, just like silver and gold is purified in the furnace (Psalm 12:6). But all other prophecies that are given today need to be tested.

The biblical canon is closed, and the prophecies that are given today *do not* add to the Bible. *Even in the Early Church, no one confused prophecies to written scripture.* The writings of Justin Martyr (AD 100–165) and Irenaeus (AD 125–200) prove that the operation of the gift of prophecy was valued and continued in the Early Church well into the third century. [5]

False Prophetess Jezebel

Nevertheless I have a few things against you, because you allow ***that woman Jezebel, who calls herself a prophetess****, to teach and seduce My servants to commit sexual immorality and eat things sacrificed to idols.*

(Revelation 2:20)

As I end the teaching on prophecy, I need to cover an important and dangerous reality. There are false prophets in the Church. Jezebel was a leader of the church in Thyatira. Jezebel calls herself a "prophetess"— *this means that she had the ability to prophesy.* Yet she was a *false* prophetess. It is important to note that she was in the Early Church. Church historians say that there were many false prophets in the Early Church.

False Prophets, Demonic Miracles, and Global Deception

> *22 Many will say to Me in that day, '**Lord, Lord, have we not prophesied in Your name, cast out demons in Your name, and done many wonders in Your name?**'*
> *23 And then I will declare to them, '**I never knew you; depart from Me, you who practice lawlessness!**'*
>
> (Matthew 7:22–23)

> *For false christs and **false prophets will rise** and show great signs and wonders to deceive, if possible, even the elect.*
>
> (Matthew 24:24)

Jesus warns about the false prophets who will rise in the last days (Mark 13:22; Matthew 24:24). There are many false prophets in our churches today.

The two great revivals of the previous century were the Pentecostal movement which began in the 1900s and the Charismatic movement which began in the 1960s. These two revivals have brought millions of people into the kingdom of God. But both *true believers (the wheat)* and *false professors (the weeds)* have joined Pentecostal churches (Matthew 13:24–30, 36–43). **It is my strong conviction that in the** *present-day Pentecostal/charismatic movement*, **true prophets are rare, but counterfeit ones abound and are gathering a massive following of well-meaning Christians.**

Waves of **false revivals** have come one after another and invaded the Pentecostal/charismatic movement, thus causing spiritual contamination among Charismatic believers. *Some false revivals are being televised worldwide.* No wonder Jesus warned that the end-time deception would be so horrific that even great Christian leaders would be tempted to follow these false prophets, who are camouflaged as prophets of God (Matthew 24:24; cf. Luke 18:8).

Pentecostals and charismatics believe that the churches today should follow the pattern in the New Testament, and since miracles were present in the Early Church, Pentecostals believe that God also performs miracles today. In the Pentecostal/charismatic movement, the preachers who become famous are the ones who can perform miracles, but Christians need to know that even the devil can perform miracles and that miracles alone do not authenticate a preacher. *I am not advocating that Christians should leave the Pentecostal movement fearing false prophets, for I am a Pentecostal Christian who believes in miracles myself, but I am saying that we should walk in discernment.*

Some Charismatic Christians are experiencing miracles as the result of praying to Mary (the mother of Jesus) and to certain dead saints. Such practices are extremely dangerous because it is not biblical to pray to dead saints. *Praying to Mary is idolatry, so people who pray to dead saints are opening their lives to evil spirits.* I write more on deception in Chapter 21 ("The Stronghold of Accepting Fake Love").

A supernatural occurrence is not necessarily a work of the Holy Spirit. *Satan is a supernatural being, and he also has supernatural power to work miracles.* The two books that helped me in understanding the deception and demonic activity in *certain segments* of the Pentecostal/charismatic movement are *Protection from Deception* by Derek Prince and *Merchandising the Anointing* by Rick Renner.

TESTING SPIRITUAL EXPERIENCES

Even the apostle Paul met with the other apostles to make sure that he was not in error (Galatians 2:2; Acts 15:28). We should scrutinize, examine, and test every spiritual experience by the following:

1. The Bible
2. Additional Holy Spirit's Confirmations

The Bible is the primary way that God communicates to us. If your spiritual experience contradicts the written Word of God, that experience is not from God. *However, you need to know for sure that it contradicts the teachings of the Bible.* This is why we should study Bible passages and stories within their context—"rightly dividing the word of truth" (2 Timothy 2:15). In this chapter, I have explained the different ways that God speaks to us. Do not override the direction that you receive from Him. There are times when I disobeyed God's leadings because it *appeared* to be contrary to the teachings of the Bible, but in the end was not. I discuss this at the end of this chapter.

When making major decisions, we need to consult with other mature Christians. If Jesus can speak to you, He can also speak to other Christians and confirm what He's telling you. Confirming the *Holy Spirit's leading* from mature Christians also validates that you are not in error (Acts 15:28).

God is never wrong. However, God works through humans who are imperfect vessels. The Bible alone has 100 percent accuracy.

THE CORRECT BIBLICAL INTERPRETATION

*Be diligent to present yourself approved to God, a worker who does not need to be ashamed, **rightly dividing the word of truth**.*
(2 Timothy 2:15)

As I end this chapter, I want to share another important point. As I mentioned earlier, there were times when God was leading me to do things that *appeared* to be totally contrary to the teachings of the Bible. I was confused. Is God speaking to me? Or is it the devil trying to deceive me?

As years passed, I understood that what I was sensing in my spirit was not contrary to the Bible's teachings; I did not know enough of the Bible to fully understand about that certain area of Scripture. God was showing me areas in the Bible where I was never instructed. My lack of biblical knowledge caused many doctrinal deviations. As I further studied the Bible, I understood that it was truly God's leadings, and it was fully scriptural. There are doctrinal differences among mainline Christian denominations. There are even doctrinal differences among various Pentecostal/charismatic circles. This is why you need to stick with the "whole counsel of God" (Acts 20:27).

If you sense that God is leading you in an area that contradicts your religious thinking, don't ignore it; God may be speaking to you. You should study the Bible further so that you can understand it fully.

CHAPTER EIGHT

OUR INVISIBLE ENEMIES

The origin of demons is not clear. Isaiah 14 tells us about the fall of Satan. Ezekiel 28 tells us the reason for his fall. The devil was not created by God as an evil being. He was an archangel, and his name was Lucifer. However, through pride and rebellion, he lost his place with God and was expelled from Heaven. One-third of the angels also joined in the rebellion against God and were expelled along with Satan (Revelation 12:4, 7–12). The leader is Satan, and these fallen angels are demons. God made Adam to be the caretaker of Eden.

When Adam sinned against God, he became a slave of the devil. Satan became the god of this world (2 Corinthians 4:4). Satan will have influence over this world until the Day of Judgment, when he will be thrown into the lake of fire (Revelation 20:10). Jesus defeated Satan at the cross. As a result of the completed work of Jesus Christ, a Christian has God-given authority over the devil and must exercise it. Even though Jesus won victory on the cross, a Christian needs to take steps to apply that victory to his personal life.

SATAN'S OPERATION IN HUMAN BEINGS

*in which you once walked according to the course of this world, according to the **prince of the power of the air**, the spirit who* *now works in the sons of disobedience,*

(Ephesians 2:2)

Who is this being who is controlling the unsaved person? It is Satan. Satan is not a mythological monster. Instead, he is a *real* prince over a *real* kingdom—Satan is the **prince of the power of the air**. He has an army of demons under him (Ephesians 6:12). Demons are spirit personalities who have will, emotions, and intellect (Acts 19:15–16). When Jesus cast demons out of humans, the demons cried out in fear and, at times, tried to reason with Jesus. Therefore, demons have the ability to reason and speak intelligently.

> *We know that we are of God, and the whole world lies under the sway of the wicked one.*

(1 John 5:19)

Every unsaved person is under the strong influence of the devil, who is the master deceiver of this world. Even though God has supremacy over the whole universe, Satan still possesses significant domination over mankind. Based on Ephesians 2:2, we understand that an unsaved person is forcefully dominated by Satan. That does not mean that the devil has *total control* over every unbeliever. When Satan has total control over a person, the person is referred to as being fully *demon-possessed.*

> *Or how can one enter a strong man's house and plunder his goods, unless he first binds the strong man? And then he will plunder his house.*

(Matthew 12:29)

Jesus says that Satan is like a dictator who has slaves and stolen materials in his house. Satan has total control over his household.

THE FIGHT OF FAITH

Fight the good fight of faith, lay hold on eternal life, to which you were also called and have confessed the good confession in the presence of many witnesses.

(1 Timothy 6:12)

Even though Jesus defeated the devil on the cross, the devil is still the god of this world, and he fights against the Christians. The devil fights our faith. If you lose your faith, you are also in danger of losing blessings that are of eternal value.

Be sober, be vigilant; because your adversary the devil walks about like a roaring lion, seeking whom he may devour.

(1 Peter 5:8)

*For we do not **wrestle** against flesh and blood, but against principalities, against powers, against the rulers of the darkness of this age, against spiritual **hosts** of wickedness in the heavenly places.*

(Ephesians 6:12)

Both of these passages were written to the Christians in the first-century Church. The word *wrestle* is used in the context of a wrestling match—a gladiator fight. The word *host* is the old English word for *army*. Christians are in a wrestling match with invisible persons who are evil spirits. These evil spirits are a highly organized army. Spiritual warfare is not optional. If you are a Christian, you are at war with Satan's kingdom. You have to accept this reality and be equipped with

God's power—because if you are not equipped, you will be devoured by Satan (1 Peter 5:8).

We are in an intense spiritual warfare with evil forces. Most Christians believe in the existence of the devil and demons. However, since demons cannot be seen with the physical eyes, spiritual warfare is not real to them.

One of the major debates about spiritual warfare is the extent to which demons can affect Christians. Some adamantly believe that Christians cannot be oppressed or influenced by demons, and the logic behind this view is that Christians have the Holy Spirit, so they are fully protected. Here is my question: If alcohol or drugs can overcome Christians, why can't the devil overcome Christians?

The World, the Flesh, and the Devil

*15 Love not the **world**, neither the things that are in the world. If any man love the world, the love of the Father is not in him.*
*16 For all that is in the world, **the lust of the flesh**, and the lust of the eyes, and the pride of life, is not of the Father, but is of the world.*

(1 John 2:15–16 KJV)

*2 in which you once walked according to the course of this **world**, according to **the prince of the power of the air**, the spirit who now works in the sons of disobedience,*
*3 among whom also we all once conducted ourselves in the lusts of our **flesh**, fulfilling the desires of the flesh and of the mind, and were by nature children of wrath, just as the others.*

(Ephesians 2:2–3)

In Ephesians 2:2–3, Paul is saying that before we were saved, three powers dominated us—the world, the flesh, and the devil. The phrase "course of this world," mentioned in Ephesians, is the ungodly culture that we live in, and the *flesh* is our fallen human nature, which is inherently rebellious against God. Before salvation, people were inclined to commit sin, but after salvation, they are inclined toward God (2 Corinthians 5:17). *The flesh is also referred as the old nature.* The old nature (old characteristics and attributes) of the believer is not completely eradicated at salvation. The Holy Spirit progressively eradicates the old nature from the believer; this process is called sanctification.

Even though Christ has subdued this fallen nature, it still resides in us even after we have been saved, but we are not forced to follow its dictates. Paul says to put off the old man and to "put on the new man" (Ephesians 4:22–24). The *two-nature view* is that Christians have two natures residing in them: the old sinful nature and the new nature in Christ. When I say that a believer has two natures, I am not implying that a believer has two separate personalities. Instead, the two-nature view describes the believer's struggle with sin.

> *I say then: Walk in the Spirit, and you shall not fulfill the lust of the flesh.*
>
> (Galatians 5:16)

Paul warns Christians not to let sin reign in their lives (Romans 6:12), thus showing the possibility for sin to reign in Christians. Christians must persistently count themselves dead to sin (Romans 6:11–13). Paul acknowledges his personal struggle with his sin nature in Romans 7:14–24. Christians are commanded not to live after the flesh, but "put to death the deeds of the body" (Romans 8:13). In Galatians 5:16, Paul admonishes us to "walk in the Spirit," so that we will not "fulfill the lust of the flesh."

THE WORKS OF THE FLESH

> *19 Now the **works of the flesh** are evident, which are: adultery, fornication, uncleanness, lewdness,*
> *20 **idolatry, sorcery**, hatred, contentions, jealousies, outbursts of wrath, selfish ambitions, dissensions, **heresies**,*
> *21 envy, **murders**, drunkenness, revelries, and the like; of which I tell you beforehand, just as I also told you in time past, that those who practice such things will not inherit the kingdom of God.*
>
> (Galatians 5:19–21)

Galatians 5:19–21 catalogs the sins that are attributed as *works of the flesh*. So, are all these sins mentioned in Galatians 5:19–21 exclusively works of the flesh? Do they have nothing to do with any demonic influence?

I picked four sins from the list in Galatians 5:19–21 that are mostly demonic: idolatry, sorceries, heresies, and murders. First, people who sacrifice to idols are offering themselves to demons (1 Corinthians 10:20). Second, sorceries always occur as a person approaches evil spirits to perform an act. Third, heresies are *doctrines of demons* (1 Timothy 4:1; cf. 1 John 4:1–2). Finally, since Jesus said that the devil is a murderer (John 8:44), the act of murder is certainly demonic. The truth is that there is a demonic element in all the sins mentioned in Galatians 5:19–21. The devil works with the flesh by intensifying its evil desires and provokes Christians to sin. In 1 Corinthians 3:1–3, Paul says that the Christians in Corinth are *carnal*, so the Corinthian Christians were dominated by their sinful carnal nature.

Our own carnal nature plays an influential role in our lives. *The three-fold avenue through which sin comes into our lives consists of the world, the flesh, and the devil. Therefore, we should not place the blame for our sins entirely on the devil.* The great danger of sin is that sin can become a habit, and the sinful habits can control a person.

WITCHCRAFT IN THE CHURCH

*Oh, **foolish** Galatians! Who has **cast an evil spell on you**? For the meaning of Jesus Christ's death was made as clear to you as if you had seen a picture of his death on the cross.*

(Galatians 3:1 NLT)

*O foolish Galatians! Who has **bewitched** you that you should not obey the truth, before whose eyes Jesus Christ was clearly portrayed among you as crucified?*

(Galatians 3:1)

The apostle Paul wrote this letter to the Christians in the churches of Galatia. There, Christians were Spirit-filled and even saw miracles, but they were also *bewitched* or came under a spell. Apparently, the Christians in Galatia had come under severe demonic attack and were totally unaware of it. Paul calls them *fools*. A person is referred to as a fool when he has no discernment—fools are easily tricked. Just like the Christians in the Laodicean Church, they were totally unaware that they were spiritually bankrupt (Revelation 3:17).

*3 And that's the way it was with us before Christ came. We were like children; we were slaves to the basic **spiritual principles** of this world.*

*8 **Before you Gentiles knew God, you were slaves to so-called gods that do not even exist**.*

*9 So now that you know God (or should I say, now that God knows you), why do you want to **go back again** and become **slaves** once more to the weak and useless **spiritual principles** of this world?*

(Galatians 4:3,8–9 NLT)

The phrase "spiritual principles" is the Greek word *stoicheion*, which means gods, ghosts, spirits, and evil spirits. Galatians 4:8 states that the Galatian Christians were Gentiles who worshiped false gods before coming to Christ. Galatia was a Roman province, so the Galatians primarily practiced paganism, and some Galatians were part of the Jewish diaspora. In Galatians 4:9, Paul is saying that the Galatian Christians are returning to "the weak and useless spiritual principles of this world," which are the so-called gods that are mentioned in Galatians 4:8. These Galatian Christians were once Gentiles; they were slaves of the devil before they came to Christ. Once they got saved, they were free from the power of the devil. By returning to Satan, they were allowing the devil to oppress them (Galatians 4:8–9). They were having a *spiritual infection*. We have to be careful that we do not open our lives to the devil. To be protected, we have to make decisions that are pleasing to the Lord.

CHAPTER NINE

THE BATTLEFIELD OF THE MIND

*How God anointed Jesus of Nazareth with the Holy Ghost and
with power: who went about doing good, and healing all that
were **oppressed of the devil**; for God was with him.*

(Acts 10:38 KJV)

From this passage, we learn that Jesus came to set us free from the
oppression of the devil. The devil is the oppressor of mankind. The
word "devil" is the translation of the Greek word *diabolos*. The word
"devil" is more of a job description than his name. In the Old Testament,
the name of the devil was Satan. *Diabolos* is a compound of the words
dia and *ballo* (or *bolos*). *Ballo* is the verb form, and *bolos* is the noun
form. *Dia* is the preposition that is attached to the front of the words
ballo or *bolos*.

There are two distinct meanings for the word *devil*. The word *dia*
means "successfully across." *Ballo* means "to throw, aiming at someone
or something." Hence, when the two words *dia* and *ballo* are joined, the
meaning is "to throw something until it is fully penetrated." The word
bolos means "to throw with a casting net."[6] When the two words *dia*
and *bolos* are joined, it describes the process of fishing with a net or
throwing a net.

DEMONIC OPPRESSION AMONG CHRISTIANS

*4 For the **weapons** of our warfare are not carnal but **mighty in
God for pulling down strongholds**,
5 casting down **arguments** and **every high thing** that exalts
itself against the knowledge of God, bringing every **thought**
into captivity to the obedience of Christ,*

(2 Corinthians 10:4–5)

The apostle Paul wrote this letter to the Christians in Corinth. Christians
need to use God's spiritual weapons to pull down strongholds. What is
a stronghold? The next verse gives some insight into it. In 2 Corinthians
10:5, strongholds are described as:

1. Arguments
2. Every high thing
3. Thoughts

The word "arguments" is taken from the Greek word *logismos*,
where we derive the word "logic." In the ancient Greek culture, it
describes a philosopher's well-calculated line of reasoning or the
convincing arguments in a debate between two philosophers. I had
a discussion with someone who was a strong believer in philosophy.
He argued his point of view that the most important thing in life is
to engage in self-improvement efforts. Once he retires, he endeavors
to become a hermit and live in the mountains for an extended period
of time in meditation. He believes that he can attain "perfection" by
isolating himself from the world. Even though his beliefs are wrong,
his arguments are convincing.

The phrase "every high thing that exalts itself against the knowledge
of God" as used in 2 Corinthians 10:5 is not just ideas. These ideas are
demonically inspired and placed in people's mind by evil spirits.

Based on the different Bible translations, strongholds are translated as follows:

1. False arguments (NLT)
2. Camps of the enemy (NIrV)
3. Fortresses (NASB)

The word "stronghold" is compared to a fortress, prison or prisoner-of-war camp. The ancient Greeks used the word *stronghold* to portray a high-quality building. A prison is built to withstand any prison escapes. One translation of strongholds is "camps of the enemy" — the devil is hiding in these fortresses. Strongholds are as real as the walls of Jericho (Joshua 6). Who is the person who is building these fortresses in people's minds? It is the devil. Some Christians are being held captive in the fortresses of Satan. How are strongholds built? It starts with a lie that Satan places in the mind of a person; some thoughts are demon-driven thoughts. In simple terms, strongholds are the lying thoughts that are *injected* into our minds by Satan. They are Satan's *thought plots* that are intended to build a wall against you. The mind is the *command and control center* of a person. The enemy wants to take over that command center.

THE TRAGEDY OF JUDAS

So [it was] during supper, **Satan having already put the thought of betraying Jesus** *in the heart of Judas Iscariot, Simon's son,*

(John 13:2 AMP)

Now after the piece of bread, **Satan entered him.** *Then Jesus said to him, "What you do, do quickly."*

(John 13:27)

The question is: How did Satan enter Judas? Satan first planted thoughts in Judas' mind to betray Jesus. I already explained the meaning of the word *ballo*. The word *ballo* means *to throw,* like someone who throws a ball. The word *bolos* means "a throw with a casting-net." It describes the process of fishing with a net or to throw a net. The word "put" as used in John 13:2 comes from the Greek word *ballo*.

The high dose of sin that Judas allowed Satan to inject into his mind turned him into a betrayer. Judas fell into the *net* that was thrown by Satan. Spiritual warfare always begins in the thought life. Instead of taking authority over these demonic thoughts, Judas entertained these thoughts. As a result, the devil built strongholds in his mind. Eventually, Satan entered into Judas.

The devil, through his craftiness, can build strongholds in the mind of a Christian; he builds these strongholds by controlling the thoughts of the Christian. 2 Corinthians 10:5 says that strongholds can exalt themselves against the knowledge of God. Clearly, this means that strongholds can blind a Christian's mind, and it can resist the truths of the gospel. As Christians, it is our obligation to cast down these strongholds.

SIN GROWS INTO STRONGHOLDS

*Therefore do not let **sin reign in your mortal body**, that you should obey it in its lusts.*

(Romans 6:12)

*Do you not know that to whom you present yourselves slaves to obey, **you are that one's slaves whom you obey, whether of sin leading to death**, or of obedience leading to righteousness?*

(Romans 6:16)

It is important to note that there are degrees and dimensions of demonic oppression, depending on how much a Christian has yielded to the devil. Yielding to the devil is sin. As long as we are in this world, we will sin (1 John 1:8–10), but sin should not dominate us. When sin is dominating us, it has become a stronghold. Paul wrote to the Roman Christians that they could become a slave of sin, or dominated by sin. Hence, a Christian can open his life to the devil and become **enslaved** in a particular given area in his life. In other words, if a Christian keeps on *habitually* yielding to the devil, the devil will build strongholds. Eventually, these strongholds will oppress and dominate him. He has obeyed the lusts of sin; therefore, sin is *reigning* in his life (Romans 6:12).

> *Then, when desire has conceived, it gives birth to sin; **and sin, when it is full-grown**, brings forth death.*
>
> (James 1:15)

This passage states that when sin is fully grown, it brings death. *Sin can grow!* As sin grows, strongholds are built. This is why Christians must pay close attention to their thoughts.

TEMPTATIONS VS. STRONGHOLDS

Strongholds are compared to fortresses or prisoner-of-war camps. Fortresses are not built in a day. Satan builds strongholds in Christians through years of brainwashing. When a person gets saved, all strongholds are not broken. The letter called 2 Corinthians was written to Christians, which means strongholds can exist among Christians. This is why we need to renew our minds (Romans 12:2).

A stronghold is not a temptation. We can resist temptation quickly. But the devil builds strongholds in a Christian's mind over a long period of time. Strongholds can begin from a very young age. Some strongholds are built because of something negative that an authority figure, like a parent or a teacher, says to the children. When parents say that their little son is stupid or their daughter is fat or ugly, this plants horrible images and affects the mind of the child deeply.

For a five-year-old girl, her parents are her heroes; she has a wide door that is open in her life toward her parents. When a five-year-old child's father tells her that she is ugly, she believes it. The parents who say such things have strongholds themselves. So, they pass the strongholds down to their children. People who are hurt most likely hurt others. Then the devil brings circumstances in their lives that will affirm the lie that was spoken. Eventually, they begin to believe the lie. Then the lie manifests in their lives.

Convincing Strongholds

And they gave the children of Israel a bad report of the land which they had spied out, saying, "The land through which we have gone as spies is a land that devours its inhabitants, and all the people whom we saw in it are men of great stature.

(Numbers 13:32)

As I said earlier, strongholds are the lying thoughts that are injected into our minds by Satan. Some strongholds are too convincing because Satan brings circumstances to prove that the lie is a fact. One example of a convincing stronghold is seen in the story of the ten spies who gave an evil report to the Israelites (Numbers 13). God performed many mighty miracles to rescue the Israelites from Egyptian slavery. Yet the Israelites repeatedly doubted God's delivering power. Even after the Israelites came out of Egyptian bondage, they had many battles ahead of them. God promised them that they could defeat the Canaanites and enter into the Promised Land. Yet most of the Israelites did not believe that they could defeat the Canaanites because their army was far more powerful than the Israelites' army.

It was true that the Israelites could not conquer the land of the Canaanites in their natural strength. But God was going to intervene and give them a miraculous victory. These ten spies, who represented the ten tribes of Israel, believed the lie that they were going to be defeated by the Canaanite armies. They had a rational stronghold of fear and doubt. However, Joshua and Caleb believed the truth and were not affected by those strongholds.

THE BATTLEFIELD OF THE MIND

The apostle Paul talks about spiritual warfare as the battle over the mind. *Your mind is the battlefield.* Satan relentlessly attacks our mind with his well-calculated line of reasoning and often defeats us. Our victories are won or lost in the mind. It is our responsibility not to yield to the lying thoughts that are brought to us by the devil. Taking control over our thoughts can only be accomplished by the grace of God and by faith. One of the practical ways that we can control our thoughts is by confessing and meditating on the Word of God. All of us have had unholy thoughts cross our minds at some point. So, we all have encountered demonic oppression in some measure.

TO HAVE FELLOWSHIP WITH DEMONS

The subject of demonic oppression among Christians is controversial. I have to admit that there are many erroneous teachings on spiritual warfare among Christians. But that does not negate the fact that a Christian can be *oppressed, afflicted, and tormented* by the devil.

*20 Rather, that the things which the Gentiles sacrifice they sacrifice to demons and not to God, and **I do not want you to have fellowship with demons**.*
*21 You cannot drink the cup of the Lord and the cup of demons; you cannot **partake of the Lord's table and of the table of demons**.*

(1 Corinthians 10:20–21)

In the first-century church, there were Corinthian Christians, who would partake in the Holy Communion and then have meals in the demonic environment of the Corinthian cults. I want you to pay attention to the word, "partake," meaning *partnership*—these Christians were partnering with demons. **1 Corinthians 10:20 says that they were having fellowship with demons**. Then, on the other hand, they were partnering with God. *This clearly shows that Christians can be oppressed by demons.* Even though the work of redemption is finished, the work of purification is an ongoing process.

Even though Jesus has done a complete work of redemption on the cross, our appropriation of the work of the cross is progressive—we are being sanctified. This is where the continuing work of *saving the soul* takes place in a Christian's life (see Chapter 6 – "The Total Man"). It is true that the new birth causes a re-creation of the human spirit; but it does not fully re-create our minds. Some believe that Christians cannot be oppressed by the devil because the Holy Spirit does not dwell in unclean vessels. That is a lie. The Holy Spirit comes to purify us— purification and sanctification is an ongoing process.

LEASING TO THE DEVIL

*Neither give **place** to the devil.*

(Ephesians 4:27 KJV)

The word *place* as used in the above passage is taken from the Greek word *topos,* and we get the word *topography* from it. *Topography* means a detailed mapping of small geographical areas, as cities and towns. Hence, you can give literal place to the devil, which means that certain areas of your life can come under the control of the devil. This does not mean that the devil has taken full possession of you. Rather, it means that you gave him a place in your life, and he will not leave unless he is *evicted* by the power of the Holy Spirit.

As I mentioned earlier in this chapter, the devil is described as one that repeatedly throws something until it is totally penetrated. The devil's agenda is to strike the mind with lying thoughts. If we believe the devil's lies, these lying thoughts can lead us to commit sins that will eventually develop into strongholds.

When a person gets saved, Jesus does not take away his willpower. A Christian can yield to the devil. Demonic oppression is a result of yielding to Satan. That is why the Bible teaches us not to give any place to the devil. This means that a Christian can give place to the devil. One *extreme* case of a Christian who yielded to the devil is the story of Ananias and Sapphira. The Bible says that Satan filled the heart of Ananias (Acts 5:3).

THE CHRISTIAN IN THE WHOLE ARMOR

Put on the whole armor of God, that you may be able to stand against the wiles of the devil.

(Ephesians 6:11)

Lest Satan should get an advantage of us: for we are not ignorant of his devices.

(2 Corinthians 2:11 KJV)

Paul wrote these passages to the Christians in the Early Church. Paul said that we need to know the tricks of Satan—we need to know how Satan operates. Paul knew how he operated, so Satan was not able to take advantage of Paul. Christians have a special armor of protection. We are required to *actively* put on this armor to stay protected from Satan's devices. If we do not wear the armor of God, we are open for demonic oppression.

ROOT OF ALL SIN–SELFISHNESS

4 Love suffers long and is kind; love does not envy; love does not parade itself, is not puffed up;
*5 does not behave rudely, **does not seek its own**, is not provoked, thinks no evil;*

(1 Corinthians 13:4–5)

*For wherever there is jealousy and **selfish ambition**, **there you will find disorder and evil of every kind**.*

(James 3:16 NLT)

James 3:16 says that selfishness is the root of all sin. If there is selfishness, there is **evil of every kind**. 1 Corinthians 13:5 says that love does not seek its own benefit. Selfishness is the opposite of love. *Selfishness is the nature of the devil, and love is the nature of God.* Selfishness is the attitude that only cares for one's own interests. Love is the attitude that cares for the interest of others. Our fleshly nature (human nature) is based on selfishness. We need to overcome it by God's love. We see selfishness in the life of Cain when he killed Abel. We even see it in the life of James and John when they were competing with the other disciples for the key positions in the kingdom of God (Mark 10:35–45).

STRONGHOLDS ALWAYS LEAD TO SELFISHNESS

Once Satan has built strongholds in the mind of the believer, he operates his nature through those strongholds. The nature of the devil is selfishness. The area where the stronghold is dominating becomes the area of selfishness in the person. It is impossible to have strongholds and have no selfishness. Satan always exerts his nature through strongholds.

Strongholds manifest by taking certain emotions to the extreme. *Strongholds transform natural emotions into a selfish demonic passion.*

APOSTLE PETER'S MOMENTS OF OPPRESSION

21 From that time Jesus began to show to His disciples that He must go to Jerusalem, and suffer many things from the elders and chief priests and scribes, and be killed, and be raised the third day.
22 Then Peter took Him aside and began to rebuke Him, saying, "Far be it from You, Lord; this shall not happen to You!"
23 But He turned and said to Peter, "Get behind Me, Satan! You are an offense to Me, for you are not mindful of the things of God, but the things of men."

(Matthew 16:21–23)

The apostle Peter had instances in his life when he was under severe demonic oppression. This passage describes one such time when Peter spoke against the crucifixion of Jesus. Peter thought that he said these words because he loved Jesus. Of course, Peter loved Jesus, but Satan put these thoughts in Peter's mind, and Peter spoke them. Notice that Jesus did not respond by rebuking Peter. Instead, Jesus rebuked Satan. Peter had no idea that he was demon oppressed at this time.

However, moments earlier when Jesus asked his disciples who He was, Peter spoke that Jesus was the Messiah. Jesus was commended for Peter's answer and said that Peter received this revelation from the Father (Matthew 16:13–19). Here, we see that Peter is flowing in the power of the Holy Spirit on one occasion. Moments later, he became a mouthpiece of Satan (Matthew 16:21–23). *It is possible to yield to God in the morning and then yield to the devil in the evening.*

> *31 And the Lord said, "Simon, Simon! Indeed, **Satan has asked for you, that he may sift you as wheat.***
> *32 But I have prayed for you, that your faith should not fail; and when you have returned to Me, strengthen your brethren."*
>
> (Luke 22:31–32)

Peter was going to face major spiritual battles. Peter did face the pressure of being sifted as wheat; Peter betrayed Jesus three times. This attack of Satan was so great that he almost lost his faith. Satan almost took hold of Peter's life as Jesus was being crucified. However, the prayers of Jesus kept Peter's life.

It is true that Peter was not born again when the moments of demonic oppression happened. Peter could not become born again because Jesus hadn't gone to the cross. Peter was still a disciple of Jesus, who worked miracles (Mark 3:14–19). The story of Peter also applies to Christians, since we are the present-day disciples of Jesus. There are so many wonderful Christians like Peter, who are demon-oppressed in different areas of their lives. Yet, they are totally unaware that some of the thoughts they meditate on are coming directly from Satan.

CHAPTER TEN

TYPES OF STRONGHOLDS

*Therefore, having these promises, beloved, let us cleanse ourselves from **all filthiness of the flesh and spirit**, perfecting holiness in the fear of God.*

(2 Corinthians 7:1)

In 2 Corinthians 7:1, the apostle Paul says that sin causes "filthiness of the flesh and spirit." **Strongholds control certain areas of the personality of a believer and cause filthiness in his spirit**. As I mentioned in the previous chapter, Christians are required to actively put on this armor to stay protected from Satan's devices. If we do not wear the armor of God, we are open for demonic oppression.

Demons can be categorized for their specific functions and are associated with particular sins. For example, a lying spirit entered the false prophets and lied to King Ahab to go to war (1 Kings 22:23).

Some of the evil spirits mentioned in the Bible are deaf and dumb spirit (Mark 9:25–29); familiar spirit (1 Samuel 28:7 KJV); perverse spirit (Isaiah 19:14); seducing spirit (1 Timothy 4:1 KJV); spirit of divination (Acts 16:16); spirit of fear (2 Timothy 1:7); haughty spirit (Proverbs 16:18); spirit of infirmity (Luke 13:11–13); spirit of harlotry (Hosea 4:12, 5:4); spirit of slumber (Romans 11:8 KJV); and spirit of heaviness (Isaiah 61:3).

All sins begin with a temptation. When we yield to temptation and commit sin, Satan will get involved and try to solidify the sin in our lives by turning it into a stronghold. Strongholds lead to compulsive sinful desires, thus disturbing human personality. In this chapter, we will look into specific cases of demonic oppression among Christians:

1. Simon Magus
2. Deliverance Ministry of the Early Church Fathers
3. Irene Park
4. Raphael Gasson
5. Buddy Harrison
6. The Stronghold of Anger
7. The Stronghold of Lust
8. Seducing Spirits

From this chapter onwards, I cite the teachings of prominent Bible teachers. However, I do not accept all of their teachings.

SIMON MAGUS

*13 Then Simon himself **also believed**; and when he **was baptized** he continued with Philip, and was amazed, seeing the miracles and signs which were done.*
20 But Peter said to him, "Your money perish with you, because you thought that the gift of God could be purchased with money!
21 You have neither part nor portion in this matter, for your heart is not right in the sight of God.
22 Repent therefore of this your wickedness, and pray God if perhaps the thought of your heart may be forgiven you.
*23 For I see that you are **poisoned by bitterness** and **bound by iniquity**."*

(Acts 8:13, 20–23)

Simon Magus, the sorcerer, got saved under the ministry of Philip. But he was not fully delivered. As Peter was operating under the gifts of the Holy Spirit, God revealed Simon's heart. Simon was still **bound by iniquity**. We have to remember that even though Simon got saved, he was still bound by his sins of the past. As a witch doctor, he had made covenants with the devil. Getting saved does not mean a person has fully been delivered from the demonic covenants that he has made in the past. Even though Simon got saved, there were strongholds in his life that were not broken. This explains why some Christians are still *bound by the iniquities* of the past.

DELIVERANCE MINISTRY OF THE EARLY CHURCH FATHERS

In a general sense, the ministry that specifically focuses on the casting out of evil spirits is called the deliverance ministry. The early Christian writer Tertullian (AD 160–240) tells about demonic influence among Christians. In one particular case, he talks about a Christian lady who went to the Roman theater and came back with evil spirits. In the Roman theaters, the actors and entertainers who were performing on the stage displayed crude behavior including public nudity. Theaters were also used for gladiator fights. Tertullian states:

> Why may not those who go into the temptations of the show become accessible also to evil spirits? We have the case of the woman— the Lord Himself is witness—who went to the theatre, and came back possessed. In the outcasting, accordingly, when the unclean creature was upbraided with having dared to attack a believer, he firmly replied, "And in truth I did it most righteously, for I found her in my domain."[7]

IRENE PARK

Irene Park, a former witch, gives her testimony in her book, *The Witch that Switched*. Even after Irene received Christ, she struggled with severe demonic oppression; the demons attacked her many times. The persistent evil spirits allowed Irene no rest. They pulled at her, threw things around her, shook her bed, and opened and closed doors around her.[8]

RAPHEL GASSON

> *31 "Do not defile yourselves by turning to mediums or to those who **consult the spirits of the dead**. I am the LORD your God. 37 "You must be careful to keep all of my decrees and regulations by putting them into practice. I am the Lord."*
> (Leviticus 19:31,37 NLT)

> *Regard not them that have **familiar spirits**, neither seek after wizards, to be defiled by them: I am the Lord your God.*
> (Leviticus 19:31 KJV)

Raphael Gasson, a former Spiritist pastor, gives his testimony in his book, *The Challenging Counterfeit*—which sold over 400,000 copies. Spiritists believe that they can communicate with the spirits of dead people. Many approach the Spiritist priests to communicate with their deceased relatives. The Spiritist priest gets into some form of meditation to communicate with the dead. As the priest meditates, he goes into a trance. Then, the spirit of the dead relative *claims* to enter the body of these priests and speaks directly to the relatives. In some cases, these priests even sound like and talk in the tone of the dead relatives, giving accurate and personal messages.

In reality, these priests are communicating with evil spirits who are disguising themselves as the spirits of the dead relatives. These demons are categorized as **familiar spirits** (Leviticus 19:31 KJV).

This is plain old witchcraft! The spirit of a dead person cannot visit you. *The story of Lazarus and the rich man clearly shows that the spirit of a dead person cannot visit Earth.* Gasson said that even after he denounced Spiritism and got saved, demons tormented him. After he had testified, the spirits tried to get him into a deep trance. They managed more than once to strangle him using his own hands.[9]

Deadly Visitations

Some Christians are being deceived by thinking that they are having visitations from *dead saints*. These *dead saints* supposedly have come from Heaven to Earth in the form of a spirit to give instructions (cf. a demon disguised as Samuel's ghost visiting King Saul in 1 Samuel 28). Some have said that Mary (mother of Jesus) appeared to them and gave them instructions from God. As a result, shrines to Mary have been built and prayers are being offered to Mary.

Here is another strange practice: I know of a well-known American Pentecostal pastor who claims that Elijah has ***appeared and talked*** to him many times, and he bases his experiences on the biblical account of the appearance of Elijah and Moses on the Mount of Transfiguration. Moses and Elijah represent the Law and the Prophets, and the whole experience on the Mount of Transfiguration was to affirm that Jesus is the fulfillment of the Law and the Prophets. After the Church was born in Acts 2, the New Testament books have no record of such experiences. **It is possible that the Pentecostal pastor's encounter with Elijah results from his overactive imagination; he may even have a neurological disorder. However, if his experience is real, then a demon disguised as Elijah has repeatedly appeared to him.**

BUDDY HARRISON

The late Buddy Harrison was the Co-Founder and Chairman of Harrison House Publishers. Mr. Harrison was the son-in-law of the late Kenneth E. Hagin. However, in 1963 Buddy Harrison had some problems. Buddy couldn't keep a job; he would just quit. He would be active in church, leading the choir, and then he wouldn't be seen in church at all. Sometimes, he would approach Hagin and blow cigar smoke in Hagin's face. Hagin knew it was the devil influencing him.[10]

Hagin was praying one day, when God told him that three demons were following Harrison. Immediately, Hagin had a mini-vision. In the vision, he saw Harrison walking down the sidewalk, three demons following him: one demon on the right, one on the left, and one in the middle. God told Hagin that when Harrison would turn to the right, he would yield to the demon on the right for the while. Then, he would turn back, trying to stay on course. He would then turn to the left and yield to the demon on the left for a while. Then, he would turn back again, trying to stay on course. He would also turn and yield to the demon in the middle. Harrison also yielded to the Holy Spirit, so it seemed as if he had a split personality. Instructed by the Holy Spirit, Hagin commanded the demons to leave. Harrison was delivered, got a job, and became successful. Eventually, God called him into full-time ministry.[11]

My personal commentary: Harrison was a Christian. Yet he had three strongholds over his mind. These strongholds were built by three demons, which were controlling certain areas of his mind. Here are the three strongholds:

1. Not able to keep a job.
2. Smoking openly, even in front of other Christians.
3. No desire for the things of God. He quit serving God.

You can readily see the selfishness in all three areas where he had the strongholds. First, he was not able to keep a job. This meant that he had no interest in working; he was lazy. Second, he openly smoked. I understand that there are many sincere Christians who struggle with addictions. But there was no excuse for openly smoking in front of other Christians, knowing that they were offended by Harrison's behavior. Third, he quit serving God; he lost the desire to follow God. All three strongholds led to selfishness in three areas in Harrison's life. Satan will always exert his nature through strongholds.

THE STRONGHOLD OF ANGER

"Be angry, and do not sin": do not let the sun go down on your wrath,

(Ephesians 4:26)

I know so many sincere Christians who struggle with losing their temper. Is all anger sinful? No, but there is an anger that is sinful. As we go through stressful situations, we can get irritated and get angry for petty reasons. Even the feelings of anger that we have during these stressful situations must be overcome by the peace of God.

However, the **stronghold of anger** is an entirely different issue. There are evil spirits who built the stronghold of anger in some believers. The worst part is, these believers who have this stronghold get angry at the people they love the most. I know a pastor who struggled with this stronghold. He would get angry at his wife and children for petty reasons. Yet, he loved his wife. When feelings of anger came to him, he was not able to control himself. He would say sharp words to his wife and kids. After sometime, he would regret it and apologize to his family.

Remember the nature of strongholds: *The area where the stronghold is dominating becomes the area of selfishness in the person.* Even though the pastor loved his wife, when he became angry, he hurt her with his words. When feelings of anger came, the only way for him to get relief was to speak out in anger. So he hurt his wife by his words for his own self-satisfaction. This clearly shows the specific area of selfishness in him.

THE STRONGHOLD OF LUST

*Beloved, I beg you as sojourners and pilgrims, **abstain from fleshly lusts which war against the soul**,*

(1 Peter 2:11)

The **stronghold of lust** binds some husbands. They demand more from their wives, and these husbands are never satisfied. Eventually, the wife gets tired and resents any form of intimacy. I want to remind you of the nature of strongholds: the area where the stronghold is dominating becomes the area of selfishness in the person.

The late Pastor H. A. Maxwell Whyte was known for his deliverance ministry. Pastor Whyte prayed for a young married man, a graduate from a bible college, to be delivered from the spirit of lust. The Pastor commanded the spirit of lust to come out in Jesus' Name, and the young man was set free.[12]

My personal commentary: This young husband had a stronghold of lust that was dominating him. If he had not been delivered from this stronghold, this young husband would have ruined his marriage. When these strongholds are broken, there may be physical manifestations. If *extreme* physical manifestations (choking, vomiting, etc.) take place during deliverance, it is a sign of *deep* demonic bondage.

After this young man was delivered, his wife said that she had a completely changed husband.[13] After all, when the husband gets delivered from the spirit of lust, the wife should recognize the change. I am glad that he got delivered. I am even happier for his wife—after all, she doesn't have to deal with her husband's selfish fantasies. Moreover, if he had not got delivered, the demonic lustful passions *might* have led him to commit adultery. The devil can also build strongholds of lust on women as well as men.

SEDUCING SPIRITS

*Now the Spirit speaketh expressly, that in the latter times some shall depart from the faith, giving heed to **seducing spirits**, and doctrines of devils;*

(1 Timothy 4:1 KJV)

*But the [Holy] Spirit distinctly and expressly declares that in latter times some will turn away from the faith, giving attention to **deluding and seducing spirits** and doctrines that demons teach,*

(1 Timothy 4:1 AMP)

*For of this sort are those who creep into households and **make captives of gullible women** loaded down with sins, **led away by various lusts**,*

(2 Timothy 3:6)

In 1 Timothy 4:1, the apostle Paul says that some Christians will depart from the faith as they become influenced by **seducing spirits**. Some people are possessed by seducing spirits that cause men and women to be drawn to them. 2 Timothy 3:6 states that these seducers are "led away by various lusts" and takes silly women captive.

Even though 2 Timothy 3:6–7 refers to men who seduce women, this does not mean that women are more vulnerable to seduction. Proverbs warns of the immoral woman who seduces men with her flattery (2:16), and people who fall into her seduction are destined for destruction (2:18–19; 7:22–23).

One of the aspects of individuals who are possessed by seducing spirits is their ability to draw others sexually. The consequences of being seduced are so severe that some Christians will *depart from their faith* and become apostates (1 Timothy 4:1).

The devil operates in progressive stages to deceive people, so the process of seduction takes place slowly and subtly. One of the striking aspects of cult leaders is their ability to seduce others sexually.

Grigori Rasputin

Grigori Rasputin (1869–1916) was a Russian peasant who hardly bathed, but he was admired by the Russian royal family (the Czars). His influence over the Russian royal family began when he supernaturally healed Alexis (the son of Russian Czar Nicholas II) of hemophilia. Apparently, Rasputin had supernatural healing powers and had the ability to give accurate prophecies. Rasputin was a womanizer, and he spent his time in drunken orgies.

As a man who hardly bathed, he had rotten teeth and foul breath— not the kind of guy women are attracted to. Yet, he had the power to seduce numerous women; he even seduced the wife of the Russian Czar Nicholas II. *What kind of power did he possess that made him sexually irresistible to women?*

> *My people ask counsel from their wooden idols,*
> *And their staff informs them.*
> *For the **spirit of harlotry** has caused them to stray,*

And they have played the harlot against their God.

(Hosea 4:12)

Rasputin's ability to seduce women was not natural because there was nothing attractive about him. I believe that he was possessed by seducing spirits that caused women to lust after him and become drawn to him. It is a dangerous thing to be romantically and physically drawn to someone who does not share your values. Seducing spirits cause you to fall in love with someone who has no merits; this intense attraction goes against common sense, reason, and logic. Without any explanation, it seems as if you cannot get your mind off this person. You are longing to be someone who has destructive character patterns that can ruin your life.

In some cases, these destructive character patterns stay hidden for a while, but as the relationship gets deeper, the hidden sins begin to manifest. By then, the victim recognizes that she was blinded by seducing spirits and has gotten into a relationship from which she does not know how to escape.

The Pastor's Wife's Affair with a Prison Inmate

Here is a story of a pastor's wife who became possessed by seducing spirits. The pastor, who had a successful ministry, starts a prison ministry. The pastor's wife joins him at the prison to minister to the inmates. Then, the pastor's wife falls in love with an inmate on **death row**. She divorces her husband to marry the inmate. Here is another fact: she no longer cares about her children. We hear stories of married people having affairs and running away with their lovers. However, this case is different because she no longer cares about her kids. It seems as if she is under the spell of someone who has great power over her will.

The Widow's Big Mistake

This is the story of a godly widow who married an unbeliever after her husband's death. Being a widow, she felt lonely after all her children got married. Since her husband had passed away and her children had all married, her loneliness led her to consider marriage again. She fell in love with a man at work who was an unbeliever. When the children heard the news that their mother was dating an unbeliever, they tried to talk to her about of it. When children asked about their mother's boyfriend, she said that he drinks alcohol occasionally, but he is a good man, and he promised that he will stop drinking alcohol after marriage. The widow went against her children's advice, and eventually married the unbeliever. Within a few months after marriage, he began drinking alcohol at home. She was upset that he was drinking alcohol, and when she questioned him, he jumped on her and began beating her. Being abused by her husband, she left her husband and returned to her children like a wounded kitten.

I can give you story after story where well-meaning people fell in love with someone who neither shared the values nor possessed the character qualities that are needed in a long-term relationship. *They thought they were in love, but they really were not; it was simply thoughts of obsession toward someone that were bombarding their minds by seducing spirits.*

It is better to discern the seducing spirits that are causing you to get romantically involved with the wrong person early in the relationship rather than to find out later after marriage.

CHAPTER ELEVEN

BREAKING STRONGHOLDS

W e are in a constant battle with the devil. I did not share the stories in the previous chapter to cause you to fear the devil. I just wanted you to understand the power and the reality of evil spirits. In the case of Judas, Satan planted the thought of betraying Jesus for money, and Judas entertained the idea. Eventually, Satan entered into Judas through the stronghold. Strongholds begin with a **lying thought** that the devil plants in our minds. All strongholds start in the thought life.

ONE STRONGHOLD LEADS TO ANOTHER

Do not cast me away from Your presence,
And do not take Your Holy Spirit from me.

(Psalm 51:11)

King David was a man who was used by God. Yet he had a stronghold of lust. This stronghold of lust led him to commit adultery, but his sinful acts did not stop there; later, he became a murderer. We see the development of another stronghold. In David's life, the strongholds rapidly grasped him. Sin can grow, and one stronghold can lead to another.

REPENTANCE

*If **we confess our sins**, He is faithful and just to forgive us our sins and to cleanse us from all unrighteousness.*

(1 John 1:9)

Here is a valid question: When a Christian is oppressed by Satan, can he get delivered by confessing his sin? To answer this question, we need to differentiate between confession and repentance. Confession is not the same as repentance. Bible scholars say that repentance is a military term that describes a soldier marching in one direction and then doing an *about-face*. When a soldier makes an about-face, he is responding to a command that was given; he was going in one direction, and then he turns to walk in the exact opposite direction.

REPENTANCE VS. CONVICTION

*9 Now I rejoice, not that you were made sorry, but that **your sorrow led to repentance**. For you were made sorry in a godly manner, that you might suffer loss from us in nothing.*
*10 **For godly sorrow produces repentance** leading to salvation, not to be regretted; but the sorrow of the world produces death.*

(2 Corinthians 7:9–10)

Repentance *begins* with conviction. Conviction is godly sorrow—sorrow over our sins. Conviction produces repentance. However, repentance is beyond conviction. True repentance means to walk away from sin and submit to the Lordship of Christ. *As long as we are in this world, we will commit sin, but sin should not dominate us. When this happens, sin has become a stronghold in our lives.* True repentance is a total deliverance from the stronghold that is oppressing the Christian—

he has fully walked away from being under the stronghold.

When a Christian has truly repented from watching pornography, he no longer watches porn—he has been fully set free from that stronghold of lust. That does not mean that he will never have another lustful thought; lustful thoughts may come to the mind of the greatest of saints. But those lustful thoughts do not **dominate** mature Christians. We overcome these thoughts by being filled with the Holy Spirit and by obeying the Word. *Christians must live a lifestyle of repentance.*

> And **do not grieve the Holy Spirit** of God, by whom you were sealed for the day of redemption.
>
> (Ephesians 4:30)

Christians can grieve the Holy Spirit. There are sins that cause grief to the Holy Spirit. So we need to repent when we commit sins. Five of the seven churches in the Book of Revelation received a strong rebuke from Jesus—He gave a strong call for repentance. For instance, in Revelation 2:16, Jesus tells certain church members of Pergamum to "repent, or else I will come to you quickly and will fight against them with the sword of My mouth."

WHAT IS SPIRITUAL WEAKNESS?

> *10 For if anyone sees you who have knowledge eating in an idol's temple, **will not the conscience of him who is weak** be emboldened to eat those things offered to idols?*
>
> *11 And because of your knowledge shall the **weak brother** perish, for whom Christ died?*
>
> *12 But when you thus sin against the brethren, and **wound their weak conscience**, you sin against Christ.*
>
> (1 Corinthians 8:10–12)

*20 Rather, that the things which the Gentiles sacrifice they sacrifice to demons and not to God, and I do not want you to have **fellowship with demons**.*
*21 You cannot drink the cup of the Lord and the cup of demons; **you cannot partake of the Lord's table and of the table of demons**.*

(1 Corinthians 10:20–21)

In 1 Corinthians 8, the apostle Paul is saying that certain Christians are **weak brothers** and have **weak consciences**. As I mentioned in Chapter 6 ("The Total Man"), the physical body expresses through feelings, the soul expresses through reasoning, and the human spirit expresses through the conscience. *When a Christian has a weak conscience, he has spiritual weaknesses.* A weak Christian is a Christian who is still connected to his past ungodly life. I speak more about the *conscience* in Chapter 15 ("When Love Disappears").

Here, Paul is addressing the issue of eating the meat that was offered to idols. Animal sacrifices were a part of the worship and were regularly performed in the Roman cult temples. The leftover meat of these animals that were sacrificed was then sold in the *temple* meat markets. Demonic rituals, prophecies, miracles, and supernatural activity filled the temples. There were also many prostitutes inside the temples. As *weak* believers entered into this demonic environment where the meat was sold, they had a tendency to return to the old lifestyle. In 1 Corinthians 10:20, Paul said that these believers were having "fellowship with demons." This also shows how Christians can be oppressed by demons, if they are not careful.

STRONGHOLDS CAUSE SPIRITUAL WEAKNESS

Yes, I am afraid that when I come again, God will humble me

*in your presence. And **I will be grieved because many of you
have not given up your old sins**. **You have not repented** of your
impurity, sexual immorality, and eagerness for lustful pleasure.*
(2 Corinthians 12:21 NLT)

The apostle Paul said that many Corinthian Christians had demonic
bondages. They were still tied to their past sins. Even though they were
saved, they were dominated by the **sinful residue** of their past. If a
Christian has a stronghold, he is *weak* in the area where the stronghold
is built—a weak Christian is committing sin in the area where the
stronghold has bound him, and the devil is enforcing his will there. A
weak Christian may have the desire to stop committing the sin—he is
convicted of the sin. However, he does not have the power to *resist* the
temptation of sin. He *habitually* falls into the area of the strongholds.
His resistance to sin is weak.

Let us consider the case of a Christian who is constantly struggling
with anger. After he gets angry, he is convicted of losing his temper and
seeks forgiveness. Does that mean that he is fully set free from anger?
There are Christians who suffer from depression; can they just become
happy by a quick prayer? Breaking strongholds is a process; I describe
it at the end of this chapter. *True repentance is being fully set free from
strongholds.*

THE CHRISTIAN IN THE WHOLE ARMOR

The Roman soldiers had well-designed armor to protect them from head
to toe. In Ephesians 6:10–18, the apostle Paul is comparing a Christian
to a Roman soldier. We need to walk in the whole armor of God to stay
fully protected from the attacks of the devil. Ephesians 6:10–18 says
about the seven pieces of the armor:
1. The belt of truth

2. The breastplate of righteousness
3. The sandals of the preparation of the gospel of peace
4. The shield of faith
5. The helmet of salvation
6. The sword of the Spirit
7. All prayer

The Bible teaches us not to give any place to the devil (Ephesians 4:27). When you are *habitually* sinning, you are yielding to the devil; the devil will claim his right to oppress you because you have given him a place in your life. The devil is an expert in exercising his rights. To be set free, you will have to repent and fight back with the whole armor of God—this is the biblical deliverance of a Christian. One interpretation of strongholds is the walls the enemy hides behind. Strongholds are built by demons, and demons operate through these strongholds. James says, "Resist the devil and he will flee from you" (James 4:7). Resisting the devil includes casting out demons (Mark 16:17). Sometimes, the fight of faith can be very difficult and tiring (1 Timothy 6:12). You need others to be in faith with you (2 Corinthians 7:6).

> *And God raised us up with Christ and seated us with him in the heavenly realms in Christ Jesus,*
>
> (Ephesians 2:6 NIV)

We are seated with Christ in heavenly places. Therefore, spiritual warfare must be done from a position of rest and confidence in the Lord. We have power and authority in the name of Jesus. Colossians 1:3 says that we are no longer under the dominion of Satan. So, you may ask, "If Jesus defeated the devil, how can Christians be tormented by the devil?" The answer is simple: When we sin, we are giving access to Satan in our lives.

BREAKING STRONGHOLDS IS A PROCESS

*For the weapons of our warfare are not carnal but mighty in God for **pulling down strongholds**,*

(2 Corinthians 10:4)

Trying to get rid of strongholds by going to *motivational seminars* can be compared to Adam's attempt of trying to cover up his sins with fig leaves. Strongholds are like monkeys on our back that follow us everywhere.

Jesus alone has the power to break strongholds. If Satan has already built strongholds in a Christian's life, he will have to seek the prayers of mature Christians to be set free. Strongholds can be compared to fortresses or enemy prison camps. Fortresses are *not* built in a day. Since it takes a long time to build strongholds, it may also take a long time to pull them down. You will have to break these strongholds one brick at a time. Just because you pulled out once, does not mean that your mind is going to be set free. It takes the persistent and consistent effort of the believer to pull it down by the power of the Holy Spirit and the Word of God.

And I also say to you that you are Peter, and on this rock I will build My church, and the gates of Hades shall not prevail against it.

(Matthew 16:18)

I am reminded of the war tactics the Mongolian warlord, Genghis Khan, used. Genghis Khan would surround the city walls that protected the city of his enemy. The city walls were massive, built to withstand an enemy invasion. First, he cut off the trade to the city. With no trade, the people inside the fortress would begin to starve due to the lack of food supplies. Then the Mongol army would strike the city walls over a long period of time. Bit by bit, the city walls would break, and the Mongol army would be able to take over the city. We can destroy the gates of hell, but it cannot happen in a day. It takes persistent effort.

Breaking strongholds can be done through a simple prayer of faith. But there are times when strongholds can only be broken as a person grows spiritually. This is seen in the case of Irene Park (the former witch). Even though Irene was saved and stopped practicing witchcraft, she was still oppressed by demons. Even though Raphael Gasson was saved and stopped practicing Spiritism, he was still oppressed.

Spiritual growth cannot happen in a day. We have to "walk in the light as He is in the light" (1 John 1:7). It takes years, even decades of faithful service to become a full-grown Christian. So, if you feel like you are in some sort of bondage, don't get discouraged. You should pray with Christians who are strong in faith. If there are weak Christians, there are also strong Christians. Try your best to associate with strong Christians or Christians who are flowing in the power of God. The most important thing is to go after God with all of your heart. Dear friend, you will have a bright future—keep your eyes on Jesus. With the help of Jesus, you will win.

CHAPTER TWELVE

WHEN SIN IS FULLY

DEVELOPED

*If anyone sees his **brother sinning a sin** which does not lead to death, he will ask, and He will give him life for those who commit sin not leading to death. **There is sin leading to death**. I do not say that he should pray about that.*

(1 John 5:16)

*15 Then, when desire has conceived, it gives birth to sin; and sin, **when it is full-grown**, brings forth **death**.*
*16 **Do not be deceived, my beloved brethren**.*

(James 1:15–16)

Sin, in the life of a believer, is extremely dangerous because sin can grow to a point where it can take full possession of a person. The sin is fully grown, and the person is fully demon possessed.

When a person becomes fully demon-possessed, Satan is in full control of that person. 1 John 5:16 talks about a Christian, since John uses the term "brother;" In James 1:15–16, James uses the term "brethren." Both passages state that a believer can commit sins that are so severe that they can lead to **death**—meaning **spiritual death**. All sins are not the same. Sins must be evaluated according to their gravity.

> *Rescue others by **snatching them from the flames of judgment**. Show mercy to still others, but do so with great caution, hating the **sins that contaminate their lives**.*
>
> (Jude 1:23 NLT)

In this verse, Jude was giving a message to Christians in the Early Church. These Christians had become corrupted by sin. Brave firefighters rescue the lives of victims who are trapped in a building that is on fire. This passage gives a parallel comparison. Just like firefighters quickly respond to save victims, we have to restore Christians who are living in sin. Fire is no game; it is life-threatening. Likewise, sin can contaminate our lives and destroy our spirit from within.

DEMON POSSESSION VS. DEMON OPPRESSION

Demon oppression happens in the mind and in the soul. Demon possession happens in the human spirit. Demon possession means the demon owns the person.

LEVELS OF DEMON POSSESSION

Before sin becomes fully grown, it has stages of growth. Demonic activity in a person can grow from demon oppression to demon possession. There are also stages of demon possession. In other words, a person can be fully demon-possessed or partially demon-possessed.

> 43 *"**When an unclean spirit goes out of a man**, he goes through dry places, seeking rest, and finds none.*

*44 Then he says, 'I will return to my house from which I came.'
And when he comes, he finds it empty, swept, and put in order.
45 **Then he goes and takes with him seven other spirits more
wicked than himself, and they enter and dwell there**; and the
last state of that man is worse than the first. So shall it also be
with this wicked generation."*

(Matthew 12:43–45)

- **Initial condition:** The man was possessed by one unclean spirit.
- **Deliverance:** Then this man was set free from the unclean
  spirit—the unclean spirit was cast out by the power of God.
- **The End:** But the evil spirit returned with seven other spirits.
  These seven evil spirits were individually more powerful
  than the first one, and when they all returned into him, he was
  possessed by eight evil spirits, and we see a much higher level
  of demon possession. *This means that there are stages of demon
  possession.*

THE STRONGHOLD OF GREED

*Now after the piece of bread, **Satan entered him**. Then Jesus
said to him, "What you do, do quickly."*

(John 13:27)

Judas Iscariot was chosen to be an apostle. He had a great future, but
sin entered his life, and he lost everything. **Judas went from demon
oppression to demon possession.** John 13:27 states that Satan entered
Judas, so he became *fully* demon-possessed.

God created man as a free moral agent, who has the right to make
choices. Man has a will, but Satan wants to take the *willpower* away
from man and enforce his will upon us. A demon-possessed person has

another person—a devil—living in his human spirit. Satan's ultimate goal is to take total control of the human being, which includes the spirit, soul, and body. Satan can only take full control of a person if he totally yields to the devil. At this point, the person has lost his will. Now the demon-possessed person has become like a machine that Satan operates.

THE HYPNOTIC POWER OF SIN

The greatest danger of sin is that it has the ability to control us. When Christians have strongholds in their minds, their thoughts are being controlled by Satan in the areas where the strongholds are built.

I like to compare demonic oppression and possession to being hypnotized. A hypnotized person is under the control of the hypnotist. Likewise, demon oppression means that demons are controlling the thoughts of the person. The hypnotized individuals have performed many anti-social and even self-destructive acts.

The god of this age has blinded the minds of unbelievers, so that they cannot see the light of the gospel that displays the glory of Christ, who is the image of God.

(2 Corinthians 4:4 NIV)

Satan is the god of this world. Can you imagine a person who rejects Jesus? An unsaved person is going to hell, and he has no idea of it. This is because Satan has blinded the minds of the unsaved people so that they will not accept Christ. Since Satan has control over the minds of unsaved people, they are in some measure hypnotized by the devil. The light of the gospel has not penetrated their hearts.

Chapter Thirteen

Understanding Mental Illness

Demon possession can cause a person to lose his natural power of reasoning. For example, the Madman of Gadara was insane and had thousands of demons in him (Mark 5). But that does not mean that all demon-possessed people are insane. Judas did not become insane when he became demon-possessed. Hitler was not insane. The Bible teaches about the antichrist, who is going to be a powerful leader. Obviously, a powerful leader has to make intelligent decisions to bring him to power.

The Cause of All Diseases

All sicknesses are not directly caused by evil spirits. However, every sickness is a result of the curse that came upon mankind when Adam sinned. When Jesus ministered healing, there were times when He spoke directly to evil spirits (Mark 9:25; Mark 5:1–18). In Luke 13:11, Jesus said that the woman who was bent over for eighteen years had the "spirit of infirmity." It is clear that in those cases, evil spirits directly caused the sickness. In some cases, Jesus said, "Be healed." In those cases, evil spirits may not have been causing the sickness.

The Strange World of Mental Illnesses

*Why is my pain unending and **my wound grievous and incurable**? You are to me like a deceptive brook, like a spring that fails.*

(Jeremiah 15:18 NIV)

The spirit of a man will sustain his infirmity; but a wounded spirit who can bear?

(Proverbs 18:14 KJV)

Some people have mental illness after they have gone through severe trauma. These bad experiences in life can take a person into a state of shock; they can cause fear, depression, and sometimes they even lead to suicide. Let us look into some specific cases of mental illnesses:

1. The soldiers who return from war
2. The Christian who was tortured
3. Escaping painful reality
4. Kenneth E. Hagin's mother
5. Physical Disability
6. Demon Possession
7. The Healing Ministry of John G. Lake

Soldiers Who Return From War

There are many cases in which, after soldiers return from fighting wars, they end up having psychological illnesses; the after-effects of war have affected their minds. Ten to fifteen percent of the soldiers who returned from the recent war in Iraq (Operation Iraqi Freedom) suffer from post-traumatic stress disorder (PTSD).[14]

In Chapter 5 ("Brain vs. Mind"), I wrote about the fact that the brain can change as the result of mental activity: This is called *neuroplasticity.* In fact, negative thinking can damage the neural structures of the brain. Trauma changes the brain and may cause PTSD. This is why the Bible teaches to think on thoughts that are pure, lovely, and holy (Philippians 4:8).

THE CHRISTIAN WHO WAS TORTURED

Our minds can take only so much pressure and pain. When a person faces unexpected traumatic circumstances, he can lose his mental stability. I know of a Christian who was severely tortured for his faith by evil men. After going through these horrific experiences, he developed a psychological illness. *However, the apostle Paul went through many traumatic circumstances, and he did not end up having psychological illnesses.* Let us depend on the Greater One Who lives in us and overcome the traumatic circumstances that Satan brings into our lives.

ESCAPING PAINFUL REALITY

Reality is so painful that people go into fantasy for the sake of escaping the pain. Eventually, the fantasy becomes more real to them, and they begin to live in the fantasy world.

KENNETH E. HAGIN'S MOTHER

The late Kenneth E. Hagin often shared the story about his difficult childhood. Hagin was raised in a broken family. His mother was a Christian. After Hagin's father left the family when Hagin was six, Hagin's mother had a nervous breakdown. Then, Hagin's mother and her children went to live with Hagin's maternal grandparents. Sometimes

Hagin's mother would want to kill herself. Years later when Hagin was in the ministry, he tried to talk about those days with his mother. As a Christian, she denied she would ever do anything like killing herself, so he never mentioned it to her again. Apparently, she had no memory of ever attempting to commit suicide. She lived until she was 80.[15]

The devil can attack the body of a Christian and cause sickness like cancer, tumors, headaches, etc. Likewise, the devil can also attack the mind and cause psychological illnesses. There are many born-again believers who struggle with insanity; it is possible to have psychological illnesses and still be saved.

PHYSICAL DISABILITY

Mental illness does not always indicate a direct attack of Satan. Instead, it could be a physical disability. The amygdala is a double almond-shaped structure in the brain, and its role is to process the emotions. The abnormal functioning of the amygdala may cause psychological illnesses. The miswiring of the certain regions of the brain may cause psychiatric disorders.

Some chiropractors believe that chiropractic medicine can treat some cases of neuropsychiatric disorders. You may look at the Appendix section (at the end of the book) to learn more about chiropractic treatments.

DEMON POSSESSION

I have to share this part very carefully. Demon possession can cause a person to lose his natural power of reasoning. *In some cases, insanity is an indication of demon possession*:

- The Madman of Gadara was insane and had thousands of demons in him (Mark 5). As soon as the demons were cast out, he became a normal person. It is clear that there was absolutely nothing wrong with his brain.

- King Saul became insane as the result of demon possession (1 Samuel 16:14).
- In Mark 9, Jesus cast out a demon (deaf and dumb spirit) from a boy that caused him epilepsy. The demon forced the boy to perform self-destructive acts including jumping into the fire and attempting to drown himself.

A close friend of mine has heard a testimony of a witch doctor who got saved and left witchcraft. This former witch doctor said that when he first got involved in witchcraft, he had to make a *covenant with the devil* to get his supernatural power. If he ever tried to break the covenant, he would be struck by insanity. He was bound by the covenant for the rest of his life.

So how did the former witchdoctor survive after he broke the covenant with the devil and followed Jesus? The answer is simple: When he got saved, he tapped into the power of Jesus—a greater power. Since the power of Jesus is greater than the power of the devil, the demons could not bring insanity on the former witch doctor for breaking the covenant.

THE COUNTERATTACK

My enemies have set a trap for me. I am weary from distress. They have dug a deep pit in my path, but they themselves have fallen into it.

(Psalm 57:6 NLT)

In the story of David and Goliath, David used the enemy's weapon — Goliath's sword—to kill him. I believe that what happened to Goliath is symbolic of something deeper: Satan will fall into the same ditch that he dug for us. This is shown in the New Testament. Satan thought that he defeated Jesus when he crucified Him, but in fact, the crucifixion resulted in the destruction of Satan himself.

> *26 But Elisha asked him, "Don't you realize that I was there in spirit when Naaman stepped down from his chariot to meet you? Is this the time to receive money and clothing, olive groves and vineyards, sheep and cattle, and male and female servants? 27 Because you have done this, you and your descendants will suffer from Naaman's leprosy forever." When Gehazi left the room, he was covered with leprosy; his skin was white as snow.*
> (2 Kings 5:26–27 NLT)

Here is a similar story: The leprosy of Naaman came on Gehazi when he tried to deceive Elisha. I can share stories of false prophets who thought they could harm Christians by their demonic power, but instead of the Christians being harmed, the false prophets were harmed. The false prophet, Elymas, opposed the apostle Paul (Acts 13:6–8). When God judged Elymas, he was miraculously struck with blindness. The demonic power of Elymas could not stop the anointing of Paul and a curse came on Elymas.

Now I like to bring out another truth about insanity: It may sound controversial, but it is true. Insanity *may* be a sign of God's judgment on the person. King Saul became insane after he disobeyed God. God had judged King Nebuchadnezzar for his sins, and as the result, Nebuchadnezzar became insane (Daniel 4:24–33).

John G. Lake's Healing Ministry

As I end this chapter, I would like to share that insane people can be healed by the power of the Holy Spirit. The late John G. Lake was greatly used by God in the healing ministry. Under Lake's ministry, hundreds of insane people have been healed. In one particular occasion, Lake prayed for a young man who had become violently insane and was admitted to a mental asylum. The doctors examined the young man and said that there was nothing wrong with his body and brain that could cause insanity. When the insane man was brought to Lake, Lake laid hands on his head and commanded the evil spirit to leave the young man. Lake could tell the evil spirit was no longer in the man when he spoke to Lake. The man was let out of the institution a few days later. He had been healed and returned to his former job.[16]

The subject of insanity is a difficult subject to write on because there is a lot of mystery surrounding the topic. My purpose for writing this chapter is to give a new perspective on insanity and hopefully see many people healed from insanity by the power of God.

CHAPTER FOURTEEN

THE DEVOURER

In this chapter, I am going to answer two critical questions about demon possession:

- Can a Christian **be** demon-possessed?
- Can a Christian **become** demon-possessed?

CAN A CHRISTIAN BE DEMON-POSSESSED?

I believe that a person *cannot* be a Christian and be demon-possessed at the same time. But a Christian can be demon-oppressed. Demonic oppression takes place in the mind of a person. Demon possession means that Satan has control of the human spirit. Since the Holy Spirit resides in the spirit of a Christian, it is impossible for the devil to take total control of the spirit of a Christian.

CAN A CHRISTIAN BECOME DEMON-POSSESSED?

*15 Then, when desire has conceived, it gives birth to sin; and sin, **when it is full-grown**, brings forth **death**.*
*16 **Do not be deceived, my beloved brethren**.*

(James 1:15–16)

*If anyone sees his **brother sinning a sin** which does not lead to death, he will ask, and He will give him life for those who commit sin not leading to death. **There is sin leading to death**. I do not say that he should pray about that.*

(1 John 5:16)

All sins are not the same; therefore, their consequences are not the same. In the above passages, James and John are talking about sin leading to **death**, meaning **spiritual death**. Writing about losing one's salvation or spiritual death is beyond the purpose of this book. But I am briefly sharing my thoughts on the subject in this chapter.

As I mentioned in Chapter 12 ("When Sin is Fully Developed"), sin can grow and cause spiritual death. 1 John 5:16 is talking about a Christian, since John uses the term "brother." In James 1:15–16, James uses the term "brethren." *There are sins that can lead to death—meaning spiritual death*. In the Garden of Eden, Adam and Eve died spiritually. Likewise, Christians can die spiritually (2 Corinthians 11:3). *Apostasy is spiritual death.*

THE GREAT APOSTASY

*Let no one deceive you by any means; for that Day will not come unless the **falling away** comes first, and the man of sin is revealed, the son of perdition,*

(2 Thessalonians 2:3)

The word "apostasy" comes from the Greek word *apostasia* (translated "falling away" in 2 Thessalonians 2:3). 2 Thessalonians 2:3 says that there will be apostasy right before the arrival of the antichrist. Apostasy means to walk away from the Christian faith or to lose one's salvation. *A person cannot be an apostate unless he was once saved.* The subject of apostasy is clearly stated in various portions of the New Testament (2 Timothy 2:12; 1 Timothy 4:1; 2 Timothy 4:4; Hebrews 3:12; Jude 1:5; Hebrews 6:4–6; 2 Peter 2:20–22).

Apostasy is spiritual death. Apostates are the branches that have been cut off from the vine (John 15:6; Romans 11:22). They once belonged to the vine, meaning they were once saved, but they are no longer a part of the vine. They broke the **covenant of salvation** that comes through the cross. A person cannot be saved and be an apostate at the same time. Revelation 2:14 says that there were Christians in the church of Pergamum who were following the doctrine of Balaam; Balaam was an apostate Jew. Hebrews 3:12 says that Christians can depart from God through unbelief, just like the apostate Jews.

Hebrews 10:39 says that Christians can "draw back unto perdition." There are eight references to the word "perdition" in the New Testament (John 17:12; Philippians 1:28; 2 Thessalonians 2:3; 1 Timothy 6:9; Hebrews 10:39; 2 Peter 3:7; Revelation 17:8,11). *In each of these cases, perdition denotes a final state of ruin or eternal damnation.*

Hebrews 3:14 says that we can only be partakers of Christ if we hold fast to our confidence till the end, so salvation is guaranteed only if certain conditions are met. Jude 1:21 says that it is our responsibility to keep ourselves in the love of God. 1 Peter 1:5 says that Christians "are kept by the power of God through faith for salvation ready to be revealed in the last time." Hence, faith must be present if we are to be kept by the power of God. Philippians 2:12 says that we are supposed to work out our salvation, so Christians need to work with God to maintain their salvation.

The teaching of Hymenaeus and Philetus caused some Christians to lose their faith in Christ (2 Timothy 2:17–18). Matthew 24:13 says that we need to endure to the end to stay saved. 1 Timothy 4:1 says that some Christians will "depart from the faith, giving heed to deceiving spirits and doctrines of demons." Jesus said to the Christians in Smyrna,

"He who overcomes shall not be hurt by the second death" (Revelation 2:11). The second death refers to going to hell (Revelation 21:8). Hence, this implies that if the Christians in Smyrna did not overcome, they would go to hell. Revelation 3:5 says that the names of Christians *can* be erased from the Book of Life. Here is the most dangerous fact of apostasy: *Apostasy can lead to demonic possession.*

DELIVERING TO SATAN

*1 It is actually reported that there is sexual immorality among you, and such sexual immorality as is not even named among the Gentiles—**that a man has his father's wife!***
2 And you are puffed up, and have not rather mourned, that he who has done this deed might be taken away from among you.
*3 For I indeed, as absent in body but present in spirit, have already **judged** (as though I were present) him who has so done this deed.*
4 In the name of our Lord Jesus Christ, when you are gathered together, along with my spirit, with the power of our Lord Jesus Christ,
*5 deliver such a one to Satan for the destruction of the flesh**, that his spirit may be saved in the day of the Lord Jesus**.*
(1 Corinthians 5:1–5)

Here, Paul talks about a Christian who committed adultery with his stepmother. Paul gave this man into the hands of Satan so that he would be judged with sickness. The sickness would cause him to repent and return to God. I want you to pay attention to the phrase, "that his spirit may be saved in the day of the Lord Jesus." Here the adulterer has already lost his salvation. If he did not repent, his spirit would be lost forever—he would go to hell. *This proves that a Christian can lose his salvation. This also shows that apostates can be restored if they repent.*

ONCE SAVED, ALWAYS SAVED?

The doctrine of Eternal Security ("once saved, always saved") assumes that a Christian cannot lose his salvation, in spite of what sin he commits. But in 1 Corinthians 5:5, Paul said that this young man would go to hell if he did not repent. Hence, the young man lost his salvation.

> *27 My sheep hear My voice, and I know them, and they follow Me.*
> *28 **And I give them eternal life, and they shall never perish; neither shall anyone snatch them out of My hand.***
> *29 My Father, who has given them to Me, is greater than all; and no one is able to snatch them out of My Father's hand.*
> (John 10:27–29)

People who believe that salvation cannot be lost often quote John 10:28–29, which says that nobody can snatch a believer from God's hand. It is true that no power can snatch a Christian from God's hand, but a believer himself can jump out of God's hands. John 10:28 says that a believer will never perish. However, John 10:27 gives the condition for not perishing: the believer has to hear God's voice and follow Him. If a believer does not follow God, he will *surely* perish.

All the promises of God are conditional. The context of Colossians 1:23 says that we can only stay saved if we "continue in the faith grounded and settled, and be not moved away from the hope of the gospel" (KJV). See also Hebrews 3:14. The keeping and the preservation of God do not eliminate the responsibility of the Christian.

> *13 In Him you also trusted, after you heard the word of truth,*

*the gospel of your salvation; in whom also, having believed, you were **sealed** with the Holy Spirit of promise,*
*14 who is the **guarantee** of our inheritance until the redemption of the purchased possession, to the praise of His glory.*

(Ephesians 1:13–14)

Based on Ephesians 1:13, the doctrine of Eternal Security argues that the seal of the Holy Spirit that is placed on the believer cannot be broken, thus establishing an eternal place in the family of God. The word *guarantee* in Ephesians 1:14 means downpayment (the part of the purchase money as a security for the rest). Thus, the gift of the Holy Spirit is viewed as an installment.

*Of how much worse punishment, do you suppose, will he be thought worthy who has trampled the Son of God underfoot, counted the blood of the covenant by which he was sanctified a common thing, and **insulted the Spirit of grace**?*

(Hebrews 10:29)

The **sealing** of the Holy Spirit is conditional because Hebrews 10:29 warns us that the Holy Spirit can be insulted, and the sin of insulting the Holy Spirit leads to apostasy. Ephesians 1:13 does not say that the seal is unbreakable. Since the Holy Spirit is received through faith, the Holy Spirit can seal us only if we remain in faith.

*And **do not grieve** the Holy Spirit of God, by whom you were **sealed** for the day of redemption.*

(Ephesians 4:30)

Ephesians 4:30 says that the sealing of the Holy Spirit comes with the warning of possibly grieving the Holy Spirit. *The same Holy Spirit who seals us can be grieved and can even be insulted to the point where the seal is broken.*

The supreme passage that provides the positive basis for the doctrine of Eternal Security is John 17:12–15, where Jesus prays to the Father to keep his disciples from the evil one; this teaching argues that the prayers of Jesus can never go unanswered. Hence, all the disciples are automatically protected from the evil one, so none can lose their salvation, since the prayers of Jesus cannot go unanswered.

Here are my counterarguments for the above assumption: First, if all the disciples are automatically protected from the evil one as the result of Jesus' prayer, why did Jesus tell His disciples to pray for their protection from the evil one (Matthew 6:13)? Matthew 6:13 should have been unnecessary if Jesus had already prayed for His disciples, and the disciples did not need to pray for their protection. Second, since Judas went to hell, Judas' tragedy can be blamed on the lack of Jesus' prayer for Judas, for if Jesus had prayed for Judas just like He prayed for Peter, Judas would have been kept. Finally, if Jesus' prayers always assured salvation and preservation, the Roman soldiers and the religious leaders who participated in Jesus' crucifixion would automatically receive salvation because Jesus prayed to the Father to forgive them as He was being crucified.

Eternal Security teaching weakens the need for personal holiness because of the false security it offers to the backslider. After all, the backslider assumes that he can never lose his salvation, so he indulges in his sins.

RESTORING APOSTATES

*19 Brethren, if anyone among you **wanders from the truth, and someone turns him back**,*
*20 **let him know that he who turns a sinner** from the error of*

*his way will **save a soul from death** and cover a multitude of
sins.*

(James 5:19–20)

James says that a believer who wanders from the truth is once again
called a **sinner**. A sinner is not saved. The apostate Christian (sinner)
can be restored because James uses the phrase "wanders from the truth,
and someone turns him (the apostate Christian) back." *In doing that, we
have saved a soul from death.* In Revelation 3:1, Jesus said that *most*
of the Christians in the church of Sardis were [spiritually] dead—a
spiritually dead person has lost his salvation. He has committed sins
that caused spiritual death (1 John 5:16; James 1:15). Jesus is calling
them to repent and get right with God. We have three passages that
show that apostates can be restored:

- James 5:19–20
- Revelation 3:1–6
- 1 Corinthians 5:1–5

THE POINT OF NO RETURN

*4 For it is impossible for those who were once enlightened, and
have tasted the heavenly gift, and have become partakers of the
Holy Spirit,
5 and have tasted the good word of God and the powers of the
age to come,
6 if they fall away, to renew them again to repentance, since
they crucify again for themselves the Son of God, and put Him
to an open shame.*

(Hebrews 6:4–6)

Some apostates will not be restored because they have become *totally* deceived and have gone beyond the reach of Jesus (Hebrews 6:4–6); *these apostates passed the point of no return.* I believe that was what happened to Judas. Whether an apostate can be restored or not depends upon how far he has walked away from God.

SATAN–THE DEVOURER

*Be sober, be **vigilant**; because your adversary the devil walks about like a roaring lion, **seeking whom he may devour**.*

(1 Peter 5:8)

Peter wrote the letter to the Christians of the Early Church. *Peter is comparing the devil to the fierceness of a lion.* Satan is looking for an opportunity to devour Christians. The only way to be protected from becoming Satan's prey is to be vigilant.

*Then Peter said, "Ananias, why have you let **Satan fill your heart**? You lied to the Holy Spirit, and you kept some of the money for yourself.*

(Acts 5:3 NLT)

Satan devoured Ananias and Sapphira, and they became apostates; Acts 5:3 says that Satan **filled** the heart of Ananias. In two epistles, the apostle Paul said that Demas was his trusted co-worker. But in 2 Timothy 4:10, Paul said, "for Demas has forsaken me, having loved this present world"—Demas was devoured by Satan. How did Satan devour him? Demas loved the present world and his love for Jesus faded away—Demas became an apostate. Diotrephes—one of the leaders of the church—was also devoured by Satan (3 John 1:9–11).

Judas, Jesus' very own disciple, was devoured by Satan—Judas is an example of a classic apostate. Even the apostle Peter came close to being devoured by Satan, as he denied Jesus three times. 2 Timothy 2:26 says that a Christian *can* be taken captive by the devil. If Christians walk away from the grace of God through *unrepentant* sins, they can lose their salvation (Romans 11:17–23; Hebrews 6:1–8; 10:26–29).

THE SOWER AND THE SEED

*They on the rock are they, which, when they hear, receive the word with joy; and these have no root, which for a while believe, **and in time of temptation fall away**.*

(Luke 8:13 KJV)

*Yet it has no real root in him, but is **temporary** (inconstant, lasts but a little while); and when affliction or trouble or persecution comes on account of the Word, at once he is caused to stumble [he is repelled and begins to distrust and desert Him Whom he ought to trust and obey] and **he falls away**.*

(Matthew 13:21 AMP)

Jesus said that His words "are spirit, and they are life" (John 6:63). The parable of the sower and the seed clearly shows that salvation can be lost. The parable is about what happens when God's Word is sown into a person's heart. Based on this parable, Jesus said that there are four types of people who respond to the gospel:

1. The first type rejects the word. They do not get saved (Luke 8:12).
2. The second type gets saved, but they will fall into sin and lose their salvation (Luke 8:13).
3. The third type are people who get saved, but they do not become mature Christians (Luke 8:14).
4. The fourth type become fully grown and mature Christians.

The second type of people received the word with joy, but they have no root. They believe for a while, but in the time of temptation, they fall away. Matthew 13:21 says that their faith is **temporary**. They are excited when they get saved and experience the joy of salvation, but the great trials of life cause them to betray Jesus. I want you to pay attention to the phrase "fall away" as mentioned in Luke 8:13. Eventually, they fall away from the gospel—they become apostates.

THE FLAMING ARROWS ARE COMING

*In addition to all this, take up the shield of faith, with which you can extinguish all the **flaming arrows of the evil one**.*
(Ephesians 6:16 NIV)

You are in a great spiritual battle. As Christians, we are in a constant battle with the devil and demons. Jesus commands us to put on the whole armor of God. Winning and losing is a matter of life and death. If you do not put on the whole armor of God, Satan's *flaming arrows* will pierce your spirit and deeply wound you (Ephesians 6:16). Just like the soldiers who die on the battlefield, you will be numbered among the dead. If you lose the battle with the devil, you will die—in shame—like King Saul. Thus, you can die spiritually, and lose your salvation.

CHAPTER FIFTEEN

WHEN LOVE DISAPPEARS

In Chapter 5 ("Brain vs. Mind"), I said that **we feel our thoughts**. Let us take the example of a mother's relationship with her daughter. In this case, the **thought** is in the mother knowing that she gave birth to her daughter, and the **emotional component** is the natural affection that she has toward her daughter. *In other words, thoughts and emotions are intimately connected.* But there are cases when the **love-based emotions** are missing in a person's life.

A perfect example of this is the mother who sells her daughter into sex trafficking. Even though the mother knows that she gave birth to her daughter, the natural affection that she has towards her daughter is missing, so she sells her daughter to sex traffickers. Here is a relevant question that applies to American society: Why do we have so many children in foster care in the US? Where are the biological parents of the children in foster care?

> *1 This know also, that in the last days perilous times shall come.*
> *2 **For men shall be lovers of their own selves, covetous,** boasters, proud, blasphemers, disobedient to parents, unthankful, unholy,*
> *3 **Without natural affection,** trucebreakers, false accusers, incontinent, fierce, despisers of those that are good,*
>
> (2 Timothy 3:1–3 KJV)

Natural affections are the love-based emotions that are generally a part of us. They are emotions that are produced by love. In 2 Timothy 3:3, the apostle Paul says that certain individuals are "without natural affection." This refers to parents who have no affection (love) toward their children. How can parents have no affection for their children? This is the result of absolute selfishness, and it happens in the days we live in. Before I can further explain why some people have no natural affections, I have to talk about the conscience.

CONSCIENCE

*Then Paul, looking earnestly at the council, said, "Men and brethren, I have lived in all **good conscience** before God until this day."*

(Acts 23:1)

*This being so, I myself always strive to have a **conscience without offense toward God** and men.*

(Acts 24:16)

*I thank God, whom **I serve with a pure conscience**, as my forefathers did, as without ceasing I remember you in my prayers night and day,*

(2 Timothy 1:3)

There are numerous references to the word "conscience" in the New Testament. The apostle Paul spoke at least three times about his conscience. In Acts 23:1, he said that he had a **good** conscience. In 2 Timothy 1:3, Paul said that he had a **pure** conscience. If someone can have a pure conscience, it is also possible to have an *impure* conscience. In Acts 24:16, Paul said that he always strove to have a conscience that does not offend God. This proves that having a clear conscience is the result of our actions. Christians do not automatically get a pure conscience.

So, what is the conscience? *The conscience is the expression of the human spirit. The physical body expresses itself through feelings; the soul expresses itself through reasoning, and the human spirit expresses itself through the conscience.*

THE DEAD CONSCIENCE

*These people are hypocrites and liars, and **their consciences are dead**.*

(1 Timothy 4:2 NLT)

In 1 Timothy 4:2, Paul said that certain individuals' consciences are dead. How did the conscience die? Since the conscience is the expression of the human spirit, this means that the human spirit of these individuals is dead. A dead person has no life. The life and nature of the human spirit are completely gone because he became *fully* demon-possessed; Satan is in total control of his spirit. The devil is living in the human spirit, so the human spirit does not have the ability to express itself through its conscience. So the conscience of a demon-possessed person is dead.

LOVE IS A SPIRITUAL SUBSTANCE

*And I will give you a new heart, and I will put a new spirit in you. **I will take out your stony, stubborn heart and give you a tender, responsive heart**.*

(Ezekiel 36:26 NLT)

*Now hope does not disappoint, because **the love of God has***

been poured out in our hearts by the Holy Spirit *who was given to us.*

(Romans 5:5)

Romans 5:5 says that the love of God is poured into our lives by the Holy Spirit. This shows that when a person is filled with the Holy Spirit, his ability to love increases. Love originates from God. Just like water can be poured into a container, love is a spiritual substance that can be poured into our spirits. Now, let me return to the question that we discussed earlier in this chapter: Why do some people *lack* natural affections? Natural affections (love-based emotions) are a part of human beings. Even unsaved people love their children. How can someone lose natural affections (love-based emotions)? How does someone lose his conscience?

To answer this question, we need to look into the creation of mankind. When God breathed into Adam, he became a living being (Genesis 2:7). He not only became alive, but he also received the very nature of God. Initially, because he was made in the likeness of God, *the spirit of Adam* had some of the characteristics of God, and he became a being that had the ability to love. But Adam was not equal to God. When Adam sinned, his spirit became corrupted, and his nature was also affected. That Divine love that was in Adam was lost. But Adam still maintained a small portion of that love and affection that he originally had. It is the spirit part of man that brings out natural affections.

Love is a spiritual substance. When a person becomes demon-possessed, Satan takes control of the whole man. Then, the spirit part of the person is under the devil's control. The nature of the devil is fully entered into him. Thus, a demon-possessed man loses natural affections.

MAN BECOMES ANIMAL

But these [people]! Like unreasoning beasts, mere creatures of instinct, *born [only] to be captured and destroyed, railing at things of which they are ignorant, they shall utterly perish in their [own] corruption [in their destroying they shall surely be destroyed],*

(2 Peter 2:12 AMP)

This verse states that animals are **mere creatures of instinct**. Animals do not have the ability to love although many pet lovers disagree with that. Because an animal is not a spirit being, it is impossible for it to have affections. Peter said that animals are "mere creatures of instinct." The dog that protects its master is simply acting on instinct and not by affection.

The fundamental difference between man and animals is not just that man has superior intelligence. The real difference is that the man is a spirit being and animals are not. *The reason that some unsaved people love their children is because, even though they are under the dominion of Satan, they are not fully demon-possessed.* The spirit still retains a portion of the nature that was given to Adam at creation. Peter talks about certain individuals who become like animals. These people have lost their natural affections, and they simply act on instinct.

ABSOLUTE SELFISHNESS

For men shall be lovers of their own selves, covetous, *boasters, proud, blasphemers, disobedient to parents, unthankful, unholy,*

(2 Timothy 3:2 KJV)

The phrase "lovers of their own selves" is taken from the Greek word *philautos.* The Greek word *philautos* is not used anywhere else in the Bible. Paul is talking about an astonishing level of selfishness. How does a person reach this level of selfishness? This is due to lack of natural affections. When these are lost, a person cares only for his own pleasure and has no room for love for another person, not even his own children.

What causes this *astonishing* level of selfishness? I mentioned in the previous chapters that demonic oppression always leads to selfishness. I want to remind you of the nature of strongholds: the area where the stronghold is dominating becomes the area of selfishness in the person. But what happens when a person is *fully* demon-possessed? Every area of a *fully* demon-possessed person is under the control of Satan. At this point, that person becomes totally and absolutely selfish. He has lost all affections and has become like an animal that acts only on instinct (2 Peter 2:12).

PSYCHOPATHY & DEMON POSSESSION

I believe that psychopathy is most likely the result of demon possession. When someone becomes demon-possessed, he loses natural affections, which can be seen in the life of Judas. The Bible clearly states that Satan entered Judas (John 13:2). This means that Judas became fully demon-possessed and lost all affections immediately; Judas lost his love for Jesus and betrayed Him for money.

WHO ARE THE REAL PARENTS?

Does the physical act of procreation alone make someone into a parent? Animals have the ability to procreate just like humans. That act of procreation alone does not make a man into a father. Just because a woman gives birth to a baby does not make her a mother. There are other responsibilities that come along with having a baby. There is an epidemic of fathers who molest their little daughters. Is the biological father who molests his own daughter a *real* father? I understand that it was his sperm that gave life. If the biological father has no natural affections, that man is only a *sperm donor*, and not a *real* father.

HONORING THE REAL PARENTS

Now brother will betray brother to death, and a father his child; and children will rise up against parents and cause them to be put to death.

(Mark 13:12)

When God gave the commandment to honor the father and mother, He was talking about parents who genuinely love their children. God did not include parents who have no natural affection and are willing to sell their children. Those parents are demon-possessed and have betrayed their own children. They do not need to be honored. Children should only honor parents who truly love them.

CHAPTER SIXTEEN

PROTECTING OUR CHILDREN

The wicked are estranged from the womb;
They go astray as soon as they are born, speaking lies.

(Psalm 58:3)

Can demons influence an unborn baby? Psalm 58:3 says that it is possible. John the Baptist was filled with the Holy Spirit while he was in his mother's womb (Luke 1:15). Therefore, just as the Holy Spirit can influence unborn children, demons can also influence the unborn. Here is a challenging truth: we know that unborn babies can be influenced if the mother is taking alcohol or drugs. Why can't an unborn baby be influenced by the evil spirits that are controlling the mother?

One of the most watched horror movies is *The Exorcist*. The story is about a 12-year-old girl who became possessed by evil spirits. I have not watched the movie and do not recommend anyone to watch it. Demonic oppression among children is not just fantasy. The fact remains that children can be oppressed or even possessed by evil spirits. In 2014, the world was shocked to see a grotesque photograph of a smiling seven-year-old boy holding the severed head of a Syrian soldier. I believe that the seven-year-old boy is demon-possessed.

I once believed that all babies and little children were *automatically* protected from demonic influence until they reached the age of accountability. But as I carefully studied the Bible, I found out that my assumption was false. We are looking into two specific cases of demonic activity among children:

1. The Deaf and Dumb Spirit
2. The Epileptic Daughter

CASE STUDY 1:
THE DEAF AND DUMB SPIRIT

*17 Then one of the crowd answered and said, "Teacher, I brought You my son, **who has a mute spirit**.*
18 And wherever it seizes him, it throws him down; he foams at the mouth, gnashes his teeth, and becomes rigid. So I spoke to Your disciples, that they should cast it out, but they could not."
20 Then they brought him to Him. And when he saw Him, immediately the spirit convulsed him, and he fell on the ground and wallowed, foaming at the mouth.
*21 So He asked his father, "**How long has this been happening to him**?" And he said, "**From childhood**.*
22 And often he has thrown him both into the fire and into the water to destroy him. But if You can do anything, have compassion on us and help us."

(Mark 9:17–18; 20–22)

The tormentor: The boy was oppressed or possessed, by a demon. Jesus called this demon a "deaf and dumb spirit." He rebuked the evil spirit, and the boy was healed.

From childhood: This demon was tormenting him *since childhood*. What has opened the door for the devil to oppress this boy since childhood? The boy was too young to commit any sins to cause this kind of severe demonic oppression.

> *15 But it shall come to pass, if thou wilt not hearken unto the voice of the Lord thy God, to observe to do all his commandments and his statutes which I command thee this day;* **that all these curses shall come upon thee**, *and overtake thee:*
> *28* **The Lord shall smite thee with madness, and blindness, and astonishment of heart:**
> *32* **Thy sons and thy daughters shall be given unto another people,** *and thine eyes shall look, and fail with longing for them all the day long; and there shall be no might in thine hand.*
> *41* **Thou shalt beget sons and daughters, but thou shalt not enjoy them; for they shall go into captivity.**
> (Deuteronomy 28:15,28,32,41 KJV)

The cause: I firmly believe that it was the sin of his parents that opened the door to the devil and led to the demonic oppression of their son. The boy who is being tormented by demons belonged to a Jewish family although the Jews had a covenant of protection from God. From this story, we can easily conclude that children are vulnerable to demonic influences, and it is the role of the parents to protect their children.

The covenant of protection: The Jewish people had a covenant of protection and blessings from God, but the blessings could only be appropriated if they obeyed Him. If they disobeyed God, the covenant became invalid. Through disobedience, they can open their lives to the devil and bring curses into their lives. However, God does not cause the curses, he only allows them. In some biblical passages, God is said to be *actively* doing certain evil acts, but God does not do evil. The real meaning is that God *allows* humans to do evil because humans were granted free will. The distinguished Hebrew scholar Dr. Robert Young states the following:

(b) Active verbs frequently express a *permission* of it, *e.g.*—
Exod. 4.21; 5.22; 2 Sa. 24.1; Jer. 4.1; 20.7; Eze. 14.9; Matt.
6.13; 11.25; 23.32; Mark 5.12; John 13.27; Acts 13.29; Rom.
9.18; 11.7; 2 Th. 2.11.[17]

I will pick three biblical passages (2 Thessalonians 2:11, Exodus
4:21, and Jeremiah 4:10) from the above list to explain how certain
causative verbs should have been translated as permissive verbs.
2 Thessalonians 2:11–12 says, "And for this reason God will send
them strong delusion, that they should believe the lie, that they all
may be condemned who did not believe the truth but had pleasure in
unrighteousness." Here, it says that God will send a strong delusion.
But the nature of God is to save people, not to sent them to hell. The
correct translation is that God will permit them to be deluded because
they did not love the truth.

Exodus 4:21 says that God hardened the heart of Pharaoh. However,
Exodus 8:32 says that Pharaoh hardened his own heart. These two
passages are not contradictory. Pharaoh was a stubborn man who
would not change, so God had to break Pharaoh's will by bringing
the judgments on the Egyptians. Therefore, God did not harden the
heart of Pharaoh, but God permitted Pharaoh to harden his own heart.
Exodus 4:21 is another example where the verbs were translated in the
causative sense instead of the permissive sense.

*Then I said, "**Alas, Sovereign Lord! How completely you have
deceived this people** and Jerusalem by saying, 'You will have
peace,' when the sword is at our throats!"*

(Jeremiah 4:10 NIV)

Jeremiah 4:10 says that God has deceived His people. But the false prophets in Israel are the ones who deceived the Israelites by saying that there will be peace. God sent Jeremiah to His people with a message of repentance, but they did not listen to Jeremiah. Therefore, the proper translation should have been that God allowed them to be deceived.

CASE STUDY 2:
THE EPILEPTIC DAUGHTER

In one of Kenneth E. Hagin's books, he writes about the marvelous deliverance of a little girl. This girl was suffering from epilepsy. Her parents were ministers and approached Hagin for prayer. Once this girl turned two years old, she started having frequent epileptic seizures and appeared to be mentally handicapped. Listening to the teachings of Hagin, the mother of the girl was convicted of a particular sin. She told Hagin that she hated her mother-in-law. Later, the couple called Hagin to come and pray for her daughter. Apparently, the daughter was having another seizure. While Hagin was on his way to pray for the child, God spoke to him. God told Hagin not to pray over the child, but rather to tell the mother that under the Old Covenant, God said to the Israelites to obey His commandments, and He would take sickness away from them and their days would be fulfilled. Paraphrasing that in New Testament, the Holy Spirit said that a new commandment has been given, which is to love one another, and by this, it will be evident that you have love for one another (John 13:34,35).[18]

God also told Hagin to tell the mother that she needed to tell Satan to take his hands off her child because she is now walking in love. When Hagin arrived at the couple's house, he told the mother exactly what he had been instructed by the Holy Spirit. Then, the mother addressed Satan to leave her child because the mother is now walking in love. Immediately, the seizure stopped, and the girl was healed.[19]

My Commentary: Praise God for His delivering power! A Christian can only exercise the Christ-given authority over the devil if he walks in love. Jesus taught that unforgiveness would open the door to the tormentors, the devil and his demons (Matthew 18:23–35). The story of this little girl is a classic example of how the sin of unforgiveness can cause demonic oppression.

FORGIVENESS IS *NOT ALWAYS* FRIENDSHIP

Just because you forgave someone does *not* mean that you need to *always* reestablish friendship with him or her. Some people are experts in *imitating* repentance—they may say, "I am sorry," but they do not mean it with their hearts. It takes godly discernment to know if the person who is apologizing really means it.

Jesus was *not* a friend of the religious and secular leaders of His time. But He loved and forgave them as He went to the cross. This should be our example. Love is *not always* friendship. You can love people from a distance and not be their friends. Jesus was not stupid; He saw the negative realities in a person's life. Love is not stupid. Love sees the negative realities of a person.

THE HIDDEN ENTRY POINT–BEFORE THE AGE OF ACCOUNTABILITY

The indwelling presence and protection of the Holy Spirit are only possible for born-again believers. Babies cannot become born again because they have not reached the age of accountability, so the Holy Spirit is not in them. Until children reach the age of accountability and accept Jesus into their lives, they are vulnerable to demonic oppression. The biblical account of the boy with the deaf and dumb spirit proves that babies and little children can be *severely* oppressed by demons—it is important to note that the boy began suffering from childhood.

DEDICATING BABIES TO DEMONS

Demonic activity will happen in a child's life at an early age if the parents dedicate their baby to the devil. Different cultures have their own demonic practices of dedicating a baby. Christians are protected from the devil's power, but *only* if we walk in obedience to God. Disobedience can lead to demonic oppression of the entire family. Christian parents can protect their children through their prayers and their righteous walk. But if the Christian parents are not obeying God, then their babies are exposed to demonic oppression. Babies cannot be *unconditionally* protected from demons because they do not have the indwelling presence of the Holy Spirit in them. However, I do believe that babies will go to Heaven in the case of death.

NEW TESTAMENT USE OF THE OLD TESTAMENT

*1 **Moreover, brethren, I do not want you to be unaware that all our fathers** were under the cloud, all passed through the sea,*
5 But with most of them God was not well pleased, for their bodies were scattered in the wilderness.
*6 **Now these things became our examples**, to the intent that we should not lust after evil things as they also lusted.*
*9 **nor let us tempt Christ, as some of them also tempted, and were destroyed by serpents;***
10 nor complain, as some of them also complained, and were destroyed by the destroyer.
*11 **Now all these things happened to them as examples, and they were written for our admonition,** upon whom the ends of the ages have come.*
12 Therefore let him who thinks he stands take heed lest he fall.
(1 Corinthians 10:1,5–6,9–12)

Notice the phrase, "these things became our examples." The apostle Paul is saying that the Old Testament's stories of judgment should be an example to New Testament believers. As the Israelites left Egypt, because of their unbelief, the majority of them did not inherit the Promised Land. The judgment of Christians over *doubt and unbelief* is a New Testament doctrine. That is why *repentance and faith* is a needed message for the Church. In the Book of Revelation, Jesus gave a message of repentance to five of the seven churches (Revelation 2).

In the Old Testament, curses were passed down to the Jewish children as a result of the parent's disobedience (Deuteronomy 28). So, based on 1 Corinthians 10:1–12, we can conclude that demonic oppression can happen to children if the Christian parents walk in disobedience.

THE PROBLEM WITH THE FLESH

7 Do not be deceived, God is not mocked; for whatever a man sows, that he will also reap.
*8 For **he who sows to his flesh will of the flesh reap corruption**, but he who **sows to the Spirit** will of the Spirit reap everlasting life.*

(Galatians 6:7–8)

The flesh represents the sinful (carnal) nature of man. All Christians have to struggle with their flesh, which wants to disobey God, even though our conscience wants to obey Him. We are commanded to crucify our flesh (Galatians 5:24; Colossians 3:5).

A Christian who lives *according to the flesh* is *sowing to his flesh*. They will reap *corruption*. Christians need to learn to be led by the Holy Spirit.

FLESH LEADS TO BONDAGE

22 that you put off, concerning your former conduct, the old man which grows corrupt according to the deceitful lusts,
27 nor give place to the devil.

(Ephesians 4:22,27)

Ephesians 4:22 says to put off the old man. As we study the context of Ephesians 4:22–27, we learn that when Christians make decisions based on their fleshly desires, a place is given to the devil. Bondages begin when we choose to live, day after day, according to the lusts of the flesh.

In the story of the "epileptic daughter," I believe that the sin of the mother's unforgiveness opened the door to the devil. She was a godly Christian minister, but she let her *flesh* dominate her. She needed to yield to the Holy Spirit and walk in love.

It is also important to note that the epileptic seizures started when the girl was two years old. I want to reemphasize what God revealed to Kenneth Hagin regarding this. In the Old Testament, God protected the Israelites and their children if they walked according to The Law. In the New Testament, we have the commandment of love. A Christian family can only stay protected by God if we obey the commandment of love. It takes more than a *baby dedication service* at the church to protect babies from demonic oppression.

STRONGHOLDS IN CHILDREN

Babies cannot get saved because they have not reached the age of accountability. Whether parents are Christians or non-Christians, their babies are not saved. The story of the boy in Mark 9 proves that babies can be oppressed by the devil. Since babies are not saved, it is the role of the parents to protect the baby. As I mentioned in Chapter 9 ("The Battlefield of the Mind"), one Bible translation for the word *strongholds* is "camps of the enemy" — the devil is hiding in these fortresses.

As we look into these two stories in this chapter, we see the evidence of strongholds. In the biblical account of the boy in Mark 9, *the deaf and dumb spirit* created the stronghold. In the case of the "epileptic daughter," it was created by *strife and unforgiveness* (Matthew 18:23– 35). Based on these two stories, we can easily come to this conclusion: The sins of the parents can leave their *little* children vulnerable to demonic oppression, even if the children are innocent of committing the sin.

THE PEDOPHILE NEXT DOOR

*2 Then Jesus called a **little child** to Him, set him in the midst of them,*
6 "Whoever causes one of these little ones who believe in Me to sin, it would be better for him if a millstone were hung around his neck, and he were drowned in the depth of the sea.

(Matthew 18:2,6)

The spirit of a man will sustain his infirmity; but a wounded spirit who can bear?

(Proverbs 18:14 KJV)

My people ask counsel from their wooden idols,
And their staff informs them.
*For **the spirit of harlotry** has caused them to stray,*
And they have played the harlot against their God.

(Hosea 4:12)

A pedophile is someone who has a sexual interest in children. Sexual abuse creates a *deep wound* in a child's mind and spirit. The **seed of illicit sex** is planted in that child when the child is sexually assaulted. Then the devil feeds the seed of illicit sex by unholy thoughts, until it becomes a full-blown tree. This is especially true of children who are sold into prostitution. After these little girls (underage sex slaves) are sexually molested by pedophiles, they begin to accept the lifestyle of a prostitute. As they are sexually assaulted, the *evil spirit of harlotry* builds strongholds in them. Even after we rescue them, there's a lot of healing that has to go on before they can become normal children.

THE PRODIGALS

I personally know numerous cases where the children of godly Christian parents live ungodly lives. The Christian parents are shocked when their children walk away from their faith as they get older. I know a pastor who has grown-up children, all of whom are saved except one—the one who is not saved is living deep in sin. This has caused much sorrow to the family because the pastor raised all of his children in a godly environment of love and discipline. So how did one of their children become a prodigal? That question is a difficult one. In some cases, Satan attacks the children and builds strongholds at an early age. As they grow older, the hidden strongholds begin to manifest and take over the person.

ANGELIC PROTECTION OF CHILDREN

Take heed that ye despise not one of these little ones; for I say unto you, That in heaven their angels do always behold the face of my Father which is in heaven.

(Matthew 18:10 KJV)

Based on Matthew 18:10, some believe that angels protect all babies and little children. If all babies were protected, how did the boy in Mark 9 become tormented by demons since childhood? How did the daughter of the pastor have terrible epileptic seizures since the age of two? There are hideous crimes that are done to children. Why are their angels not protecting them?

We are living in a world of sin, where Satan is god (2 Corinthians 4:4). It is the primary responsibility of the parents to protect their children from demonic power. However, if the parents are not living a life that is obedient to God, their little children are open to demonic attacks. *An angel does not have more right over a child than the parents.*

There is an aspect of the sovereignty of God in which God can intervene in the lives of children, in spite of the sins of the parents. Those cases of the sovereign acts of God are beyond human comprehension. However, in a general sense, God's blessings come to children as a result of the godliness and obedience of the parents.

CHAPTER SEVENTEEN

GENERATIONAL CURSES:

MYTH OR TRUTH?

*You shall not bow down to them or serve them; for I, the Lord your God, am a jealous God, **visiting the iniquity of the fathers upon the children to the third and fourth generations** of those who hate Me,*

(Deuteronomy 5:9 AMP)

The teaching on **generational curses** was popularized by the internationally recognized Bible scholar, Derek Prince. This teaching is a debatable subject among Bible scholars. In this chapter, I take a balanced approach to the subject. Generational curses are the sins of the parents, passed down through the next few generations (Exodus 20:5; 34:7; Numbers 14:18; Deuteronomy 5:9).

First, what are curses? Curses are the penalties received due to committing sin. Deuteronomy 5:9 says that the "iniquity of the fathers" will be passed down to the third and fourth generations. God is saying that when people sinned against God, their sins were passed down to their children, grandchildren, and great-grandchildren. *Deuteronomy 5:9 implies that sin is both hereditary and personal. Generational curses are a result of disobedience to God by God's covenant people.*

GENERATIONAL SINS

I prefer to distinguish between **generational curses** and **generational sins**. I believe that generational sins is one aspect of generational curses. Generational sins occur when a person is **predisposed** to follow certain negative character patterns of his or her ancestors. In other words, a person has a **tendency** to follow certain negative character patterns that some of his or her ancestors may have also had. Let us consider the case of uncontrollable anger: The son has the same uncontrollable anger that the father has. Or the son of a drunkard becomes a drunkard just like his father. The children repeat the sins of the parents. The reason behind this is that the evil spirits that oppressed the parents also oppress the children.

In the previous chapter, I explained that demonic oppression could happen even for unborn children. Hence, the devil can place his hands on the unborn. I believe that in cases of demon-possessed people like Hitler, the devil's hand might have been on them even when they were in their mother's womb.

Generational curses do not always have to be demonic. Instead, they could be **soulish** predispositions that are passed down. The **nature and nurture** of a family molds one's personality. *Recent research proves that behavioral disorders (mental health conditions) can be passed down through the genes.*

THE SIN OF KING DAVID

When David killed Uriah, the spiritual covering over David's children was removed. David's sin allowed his children to be heavily influenced by evil spirits, and a curse was passed on to his children (2

Samuel 12:10–12). Therefore, David's sin began a generational curse of murder in his family. David's son, Absalom, became a murderer. The spirit of murder that influenced David was passed to Absalom. Keep in mind that even though David repented, evil spirits still possessed Absalom. Absalom never repented from his sins.

Here is an important question regarding generational curses: *When Christian parents are disobedient to God, can the act of disobedience bring curses to the children, just as it happened in Old Testament times?*

CASE STUDY 1: THE DEAF AND DUMB SPIRIT

Let us go back to the story of the boy with the deaf and dumb spirit (Mark 9:20–22). I discussed this in the previous chapter. How did this Jewish boy become oppressed by evil spirits from a young age? What deadly sins can a little boy commit to open the door to the devil? It is totally unreasonable to believe that the boy committed sins that triggered the curse. It has to be the sins of the parents or the ancestors that caused the curse. It is important to see that the parents were not oppressed by the deaf and dumb spirit, but a curse was passed on to the boy.

CASE STUDY 2: THE EPILEPTIC DAUGHTER

The story of the epileptic daughter (as discussed in the previous chapter) is another example of demons attacking children from a young age. The little girl had been having epileptic seizures since she was two years old. The mother's sin of unforgiveness is what caused the curse for her two-year-old daughter. The apostle Paul said that the Old Testament's stories of judgment should be an example to New Testament believers (1 Corinthians 10:1–12). The children can suffer from the disobedience of the Christian parents. The mother was living in strife, and the child was attacked with epileptic seizures. We are seeing a cause-and-effect situation. Notice that the mother did not have epileptic seizures. But the sin of the mother opened the door for the devil to attack her daughter. The story of the boy with the deaf and dumb spirit is a very similar case. The little boy is attacked, and not the parents. However, I firmly believe that the sins of the parents caused the demons to attack their little son. This shows that little children can become victims of generational curses.

JEZEBEL'S CHILDREN

*And unto the **angel** of the church in Thyatira write; These things saith the Son of God, who hath his eyes like unto a flame of fire, and his feet are like fine brass;*

(Revelation 2:18 KJV)

Jesus appeared to the apostle John to give a message to the church in Thyatira. The apostle John was probably the general overseer of all seven churches that are mentioned in the Book of Revelation. The word *angel* is from the Greek word, *aggelos*. However, in Mark 1:2, Luke 7:24, Luke 9:52, and James 2:25, it means *human messengers*. The word *aggelos* does not represent a heavenly being in this context. After all, why would Jesus appear to John and tell him to give a message to a supernatural being? Moreover, if Jesus was giving a message to supernatural beings (angels), then the angels were being rebuked for the sins of the churches. Here we see that Jesus was addressing the *human messengers*—the pastors.

*20 Nevertheless I have a few things against you, because you allow **that woman Jezebel**, who calls herself a prophetess, to*

teach and seduce My servants to commit sexual immorality and
eat things sacrificed to idols.
*23 **I will kill her children with death**, and all the churches shall*
know that I am He who searches the minds and hearts. And I
will give to each one of you according to your works.

(Revelation 2:20,23)

Jezebel was active and had a great influence in the church of Thyatira, but she was a false prophetess. If Jezebel's children were once saved, but became spiritually contaminated as the result of their mother's influence, it would be a New Testament example of a generational curse: Jesus said, "I will kill her children with death." The children yielded to the evil spirits in their mother. Hence, the children of Jezebel followed the sins of their mother. Jesus said that the children will be judged along with the mother.

THE CASE FOR GENERATIONAL CURSES

Can a born-again believer have generational curses? Some believe that when a person gets saved, all curses are automatically broken because "old things are passed away; behold, all things are become new" (2 Corinthians 5:17). However, what is the real meaning behind 2 Corinthians 5:17? What old things have passed away, and what things are new? This statement means that the human spirit is reborn; when a person gets saved, he is born into the family of God.

When we become born again, we are delivered from the penalty of sin. Subsequently, in an ongoing way, we are being delivered from the power of sin. *In some cases, all curses can be broken at the moment a person gets saved. In other cases, it is a process.*

Yes, I am afraid that when I come again, God will humble me

*in your presence. **And I will be grieved because many of you
have not given up your old sins**. You have not repented of your
impurity, sexual immorality, and eagerness for lustful pleasure.*
(2 Corinthians 12:21 NLT)

*22 that you **put off, concerning your former conduct, the old
man which grows corrupt according to the deceitful lusts**,
23 and be renewed in the spirit of your mind,*
(Ephesians 4:22–23)

Christians can have strongholds and be tied to their past sins (2 Corinthians 12:20–21). These past sins may include the sinful patterns that a person exhibited before he or she got saved, or the sinful pattern that a person exhibited after he or she got saved. Even after we get saved, we are still required to renew our minds (Romans 12:2). Ephesians 4:22–23 says that we need to put away the sins of the former life (the life we lived before salvation). The next argument is that if the children commit the sins of the parents, it is simply a learned behavior of the children.

In 1 Corinthians 10:6–11, the apostle Paul says that the Old Testament's stories of judgment should be an example to New Testament believers (see explanation in the previous chapter). As the Israelites left Egypt, because of their unbelief, the majority of them did not inherit the Promised Land. The judgment of Christians over disobedience is a New Testament doctrine. As I mentioned earlier, generational curses originated when God's covenant people were disobedient. Let us consider the story of the epileptic daughter from the previous chapter (Case Study 2): The story proves that when Christian parents are disobedient to God, the act of disobedience can bring curses to the children, just as it happened in Old Testament times.

Do I Have a Curse?

No curse can touch Jacob; no magic has any power against Israel. For now it will be said of Jacob, 'What wonders God has done for Israel!'

(Numbers 23:23 NLT)

Here is an important question: Will I be judged for my parents' sins? There is always a strong tendency to follow the character patterns of the parents. When children are raised in an environment in which their *Christian/Non-Christian* parents are constantly yielding to the devil, the demons that are oppressing the parents will eventually build strongholds in the children. *Recent research proves that behavioral disorders can be passed through the genes.* You will have a much greater temptation to commit the particular sins that are attached to your parents.

The NIV version of Deuteronomy 5:9 says "punishing the children for the sin of the parents." The sins of the parents give demons access to attack their children with strong temptations to commit sins. When King David sinned, the spiritual covering over his family was removed, so his children also sinned. Likewise, when parents sin against God, the spiritual covering over the children are removed. However, it does not matter what sin your parents committed, you can choose to obey God. You can defeat the powerful temptations that Satan brings by the power of the Holy Spirit. In other words, you have a real fight with demons, and you have to put on the whole armor of God to win the battle. However, if you fully obey God, you will not be affected.

CHAPTER EIGHTEEN

THE RECURRING SIN

*20 For if, after they have escaped the pollutions of the world through the knowledge of the Lord and Savior Jesus Christ, **they are again entangled in them** and overcome, the latter end is worse for them than the beginning.*

21 For it would have been better for them not to have known the way of righteousness, than having known it, to turn from the holy commandment delivered to them.

*22 But it has happened to them according to the true proverb: "**A dog returns to his own vomit**," and, "a sow, having washed, to her wallowing in the mire."*

(2 Peter 2:20–22)

So many Christians backslide, which means they go back to the sinful practices of their past lives (2 Peter 2:20–22). There are alcoholics and drug addicts who got delivered from their addictions after they became Christians. But after a while, they left both God and the church and became alcoholics and drug addicts again. Others went back to their past immoral lifestyle. What is really happening here? It seems like the sins have returned, or is it that they have returned to their sins?

The Ex-Alcoholic

I want to share a story about an evangelist, who, before he got saved, was an alcoholic. When he came to Christ, he was completely delivered from his alcohol addiction. He began to minister to others and had great results. On one occasion, he happened to be in a bar witnessing to someone. The person next to him was drinking alcohol. When the waiter placed an empty glass (cup) in front of the evangelist to serve him alcohol, he suddenly felt the urge to drink. He began to touch and rub the cup. He recognized that he was being drawn back into drinking alcohol, so he got up and left the bar.

This is what happened: In the life of this evangelist, the **stronghold of alcohol addiction** was not fully broken. Satan was bringing those demonic thoughts back into his life. The cravings for alcohol that this evangelist had before he got saved were dormant in him. The addiction to alcohol that he once had became a **predisposition**, or tendency, to crave alcohol. The environment of the bar activated the dormant cravings that were already in him. So the desire for alcohol returned to him.

The Ex-Boyfriend

Here is a story about a pastor's wife who was tempted to commit adultery with her ex-boyfriend. Before dating and getting married to her current husband, she had a boyfriend whom she hadn't seen in many years. Then, she came across her ex-boyfriend and got reacquainted with him. As they began talking, the ex-boyfriend started to share with the pastor's wife the problems he was having in his marriage. The pastor's wife wanted to help him, so she began to counsel him. Eventually, she started having feelings for her ex-boyfriend, to the point that she was tempted to commit adultery. Then, she recognized the danger and ended the relationship.

This is what happened: Because she once had a strong relationship with her ex-boyfriend, soul ties (emotional bonds between two friends) were built between them. So when she got reacquainted with him, and he began to share his marital problems with her, she became emotionally attached to him all over again. This revived the thoughts and feelings that she once had for him, and Satan began to strike her mind with thoughts of lust to commit adultery.

KING DAVID'S INQUIRIES

*Therefore David **inquired** of the Lord, saying, "Shall I go and attack these Philistines?" And the Lord said to David, "Go and attack the Philistines, and save Keilah."*

(1 Samuel 23:2)

God anointed David to be king over Israel when he was a teenager. When he killed Goliath, everyone in Israel knew that God's hand was on David. The period between when he was anointed and the time he actually became king was 13–15 years. During this period, from being anointed to becoming king, David fought many battles, and on numerous occasions his life was at risk. But David knew that he would become king. One of the unique characteristics of David is that before he went to war, he always inquired of the Lord. In some cases, God gave specific strategies for war.

If David was already anointed to be king, why should he inquire of the Lord before he went to war? David knew that the prophecy over his life would only be fulfilled if he closely followed the instructions from God. Let us learn from the life of King David. *I believe that we should only minister to others as the Holy Spirit leads us.*

CAUTION FOR PREACHERS!

*Stand fast therefore in the liberty by which Christ has made us free, and **do not be entangled again with a yoke of bondage.***

(Galatians 5:1)

We have looked into the life of two preachers who *almost* fell into sin as they tried to minister to others. They were not prepared for the onslaught of the enemy. In the story of the pastor's wife, we see that she started off with sincere intentions, but she became vulnerable to sexual temptation. There are tragic cases where the preachers themselves committed adultery while attempting to help others get free from bondage because they developed an *unhealthy* closeness or affinity. I believe that *some* pastors failed morally due to deception instead of an intentional planned attempt to commit the sin. They thought that the feelings they had (like the pastor's wife) were a result of their compassion toward the ones who approached for prayer, and eventually those feelings became corrupted and lustful.

Unless you have *fully* consecrated your life to God, there are thoughts and cravings in your soul that are dormant in you from your past sinful life. These dormant thoughts are **pockets of bondage** that are in the mind. Unfortunately, certain circumstances can activate the dormant thoughts and cravings. *Only God knows your weaknesses.* Do not go beyond the measure of your faith and fall into the trap of the enemy. Your passion for ministering to others must be accompanied by the leadings of the Holy Spirit.

Therefore I run thus: not with uncertainty. Thus I fight: not as one who beats the air.

(1 Corinthians 9:26)

The apostle Paul fought the devil and struck him over and over on his face. The secret of Paul's success was that he always followed the leadings of the Holy Spirit. We can only defeat the devil if we follow the leadings of the Holy Spirit. There are preachers who have had nervous breakdowns after they stepped into ministry. I did not write this chapter to discourage anyone from entering into full-time ministry. Being in full-time ministry is a real fight; you are threatening the devil's domain, and he will fight back. Having a close combat fight with the devil is no Disneyland experience.

> *Dear brothers and sisters, if another believer is overcome by some sin, you who are godly should gently and humbly help that person back onto the right path. **And be careful not to fall into the same temptation yourself**.*
>
> (Galatians 6:1 NLT)

In Galatians 6:1, Paul warns Christians about falling into temptation while ministering to others. There are preachers who were once well known, but they fell into sin, and are not recognized anymore. Here is my piece of advice for preachers: Be a slow beginner and a strong finisher. Ministry is not a sprint; it is a marathon.

CHAPTER NINETEEN

DEFILEMENT THROUGH

FORBIDDEN FRIENDS

*11 Not what goes into the mouth **defiles** a man; but what comes out of the mouth, this **defiles** a man."*
*18 But those things which proceed out of the mouth come from the heart, and they **defile** a man.*
19 For out of the heart proceed evil thoughts, murders, adulteries, fornications, thefts, false witness, blasphemies.

(Matthew 15:11,18–19)

In John 13:10–11, Jesus said to the disciples that they were all clean except Judas. When a person is oppressed by demons, he is defiled. As we saw earlier, Judas had a stronghold of greed. This caused him to eventually betray Jesus. Jesus was not referring to a physical defilement. It is a spiritual reality. In the life of Judas, defilement began in his mind, then entered into his spirit.

THE YEAST INFECTION

*6 Your glorying is not good. **Do you not know that a little***

leaven leavens the whole lump?
7 Therefore purge out the old leaven, that you may be a new
lump, since you truly are unleavened. For indeed Christ, our
Passover, was sacrificed for us.

(1 Corinthians 5:6–7)

A little leaven leavens the whole lump.

(Galatians 5:9)

In 1 Corinthians 5, the apostle Paul addresses a serious problem—a
man is having an affair with his stepmother. Paul compares the sin of
this man to that of the effect of yeast. Just like yeast spreads quickly
through the dough, sin can spread rapidly in the Church through the
wrong association. If the man does not repent, his sin will penetrate the
entire church. The stronghold of lust that operates through his life will
attach itself to the rest of the members of the church.

DEFILEMENT THROUGH WRONG
RELATIONSHIPS

But we command you, brethren, in the name of our Lord Jesus
Christ, that you withdraw from every brother who walks
disorderly and not according to the tradition which he received
from us.

(2 Thessalonians 3:6)

*But now I have written to you **not to keep company with anyone***
***named a brother,** who is sexually immoral, or covetous, or an*
idolater, or a reviler, or a drunkard, or an extortioner—not even
to eat with such a person.

(1 Corinthians 5:11)

*Don't be fooled by those who say such things, for "**bad company corrupts good character.**"*

(1 Corinthians 15:33 NLT)

The devil is looking for ways to penetrate the life of a Christian. *One of the ways that Satan defiles us is through wrong relationships.* Your friends will always have a strong influence on your life; many good people have ruined their lives because of wrong friendships. In 2 Thessalonians 3:6, Paul **commands** us to stay away from Christians who are living in sin. Notice that Paul used the word "command," and is not just recommending this action.

A committed Christian should not have close fellowship with a compromising Christian. James 4:4 says that a Christian who is a "friend of the world" is an enemy of God. There are many Christians whose lives are not pleasing to God. Even though they are saved, they are **enemies** of God. Associating with such Christians can defile a committed Christian. There is an old saying, "Birds of a feather flock together," which simply means that people who have similar characteristics or interests will often choose to spend time together; it also means that you become like your friends. Sometimes, we form wrong friendships. Unless you are *unusually* strong, wrong friends can misguide you.

There are some people who falsely assume that they are spiritual giants. Then, there are the *genuine* spiritual giants. God gave me the privilege to have close fellowship with a couple of genuine spiritual giants who all have one common characteristic: They choose their friends very carefully. Some sincere Christians have fallen into deception through counterfeit friendships. These Christians became defiled as the evil spirits who were oppressing the counterfeit friends began to attach themselves to the sincere Christians. The devil got access into the lives of good Christians through wrong relationships.

Like Father, Like Son

And a man's foes shall be they of his own household.
(Matthew 10:36 KJV)

The fastest way that defilement happens to children is through parents, relatives, and classmates. Let's face the facts: There are demon-possessed individuals in this world; and they are fathers, mothers, uncles, aunts, sisters, brothers, and cousins. Why do some children follow the evil practices of their parents? The reason is defilement through associations.

As children are raised in a demonic environment in their homes, the evil spirits who were oppressing the parents eventually attach to the children. Some parents have foolishly allowed their children to spend time with ungodly relatives. Children are fragile, and they do not have discernment. Parents should not allow their children to hang around with ungodly relatives or even certain professing Christians.

As I wrote in Chapter 9 ("The Battlefield of the Mind"), there are many well-meaning Christians who have strongholds—the apostle Paul describes these Christians as *weak* brothers. When children are raised in an environment in which their *weak* Christian parents are constantly yielding to the devil, these demons will eventually build strongholds in the children. The ungodly atmosphere in the home establishes points of bondage in children. No wonder we have so many Christian teenagers who are into all sorts of wrongdoing. Most likely they got it from their relatives and classmates.

Walking Idols

14 *Be ye not unequally yoked together with unbelievers*: *for what **fellowship** hath righteousness with unrighteousness? and* *what **communion** hath light with darkness?*

15 And what concord hath Christ with Belial? or what part hath he that believeth with an infidel?

*16 **And what agreement hath the temple of God with idols**? for ye are the temple of the living God; as God hath said, I will dwell in them, and walk in them; and I will be their God, and they shall be my people.*

17 Wherefore come out from among them, and be ye separate, saith the Lord, and touch not the unclean thing; and I will receive you.

18 And will be a Father unto you, and ye shall be my sons and daughters, saith the Lord Almighty.

1 Having therefore these promises, dearly beloved, let us cleanse ourselves from all filthiness of the flesh and spirit, perfecting holiness in the fear of God.

(2 Corinthians 6:14–7:1 KJV)

2 Corinthians 6:14 says that Christians are not to be **"unequally yoked"** with unbelievers. **But who are these "unbelievers"?** In 2 Corinthians 6:14–16, Paul is classifying individuals as belonging to two extreme camps: Temple of the living God or idols. In verse 16 and 17, the believer is identified as the temple of the living God. Since a believer has the Holy Spirit living inside him, he is the temple of God (cf. 1 Corinthians 3:16). The unbeliever is identified as the idol. Idolatry denotes the worship of images and the worship of false gods. Pagan devotees believed that their deity indwells in the idol. However, when people pray to idols, they are praying to demons (Deut. 32:16–17).

Just like demons can inhibit in an idol to get the praise of people, demons can inhibit in humans. In fact, the ultimate aim of demons is to inhibit in humans. **The unbelievers mentioned in 2 Corinthians 6:14–16 are not all unbelievers; instead, they are the unbelievers**

who are demon-possessed. As I described in previous chapters, a demon-possessed person has demons living in him. Paul compares these unbelievers to idols. **Since demons live in a demon-possessed individual, the demon-possessed person is a "walking idol."** The "walking idol" is more dangerous than an idol in a pagan temple. After all, an idol in a pagan temple mostly influences the people who worship the idol. However, the "walking idol"(the demon-possessed individual) can influence you, if you become his friend. The common thread between the demon-possessed individual and an idol is that demons live in both of them.

Paul's usage of "yoking" conveys the idea of two animals joined at the neck plowing the field. The most popular view is that the passage is a prohibition of the marriage between a believer and an unbeliever (mixed marriage). However, the passage has more than one application. Verse 14 uses two other words to describe what it means to yoke to one another: "fellowship" and "communion." Sure, fellowship and communion happen in marriage. Apart from the prohibition of mixed marriage, this passage also has to do with the prohibition of establishing close friendships with demon-possessed individuals. Christians should not have close friendships with demon-possessed individuals. Verse 17 warns Christians to separate from these unbelievers. 2 Corinthians 6:14–7:1 forms a definite unit. In the closing exhortation at 2 Corinthians 7:1, Paul says that Christians who violated 2 Corinthians 6:14 must be cleansed from spiritual defilement.

All unbelievers are not demon-possessed. Some demon-possessed people are wolves in sheep's clothing and appear innocent. Satan is the god of this world and has possessed millions of people around the world. **I must warn you: some of your relatives may be demon–possessed. This is one reason why Jesus said a man's enemy is his own household (Matthew 10:36). You need to have the supernatural wisdom of God to deal with demon-possessed relatives.**

CHAPTER TWENTY

DON'T ACCEPT THEIR LOVE!

Beloved, do not believe every spirit, but test the spirits, whether they are of God; because many false prophets have gone out into the world.

(1 John 4:1)

*Don't be fooled by those who say such things, for "**bad company corrupts good character**."*

(1 Corinthians 15:33 NLT)

After graduating from college, I started working as an accountant in Houston. While I was working, God spoke to me to leave my job; He was calling me into full-time ministry. Once I left my job, I spent a few months in prayer. Then, I started preaching. To my amazement, I saw many miracles happen through my ministry. People were healed and delivered by the power of God. Then I joined Christ for the Nations Institute in Dallas, Texas. *In this chapter, I am repeating the story I wrote in the introduction of this book to bring further clarity.*

THE VISION

While I was studying at the Bible school, I had a few experiences that I would like to share. One day while praying, I saw a vision: In this vision, I saw a close friend of mine, a professing Christian, trying to hang me. At that time, I rarely saw visions; I was shocked by it and didn't understand what it meant. This vision was not a result of my imagination because I would never have imagined that my close friend would attempt to kill me. This was very confusing to me because the person I saw in the vision appeared to be very nice. But I knew that the vision was from God.

The Hidden Reality

The heart is deceitful above all things, and desperately wicked: who can know it?

(Jeremiah 17:9 KJV)

Somebody said, "truth is stranger than fiction," meaning that reality can be more bizarre than anything that can be imagined. During the subsequent years, I came to know that this person had a history of psychological illness, which of course I didn't know about when I saw the vision. The miswiring of the certain regions of the brain may cause psychological illnesses. However, that was not the reason for this person's mental condition. The Bible shows that in some cases, these disorders are connected to demons, as seen in the biblical account of the madman of Gadara (Mark 5).

There were some rare occasions when this person I saw in the vision had extreme and dangerous character fluctuations: He could turn into another person and deeply hurt others. However, he did not have *Multiple Personality Disorder.* There were times when his actions proved that he did not have any conscience or natural affections, and he expressed *absolute* selfishness. For the most part, he appeared to be godly and an extremely spiritual person.

If you had met him, you would have never noticed that he had any kind of mental disorder. For 99.9 percent of the time, he was normal. It appeared as though he had a conscience for that part of the time, but for the other 0.01 percent, there was no conscience. I was absolutely shocked when I came to know about his *extreme* and dangerous character fluctuations. I never expected that someone who *appeared* to be a deeply spiritual person could have a strong demonic nature. If I had known about it, I would have stayed away. For the sake of protecting the identity of this person, I am not going into any further details.

A Surprise Attack

Now, let us go back to the vision. I knew that God was speaking to me, but I did not understand the full meaning of the vision, and I didn't take it seriously. After a few weeks, I received a phone call from this person I saw in the vision and had a short chat with him over the phone. The next night, tragedy struck—I couldn't sleep! I was shocked. I think I eventually fell asleep around 6 am and woke up after an hour. This was a strange experience for me. Some people suffer from insomnia due to stress, but I was not in any stressful situation that might cause me to lose sleep. This life of sleeplessness later developed into a pattern; from then on, I only slept a few hours every day. Then I remembered the warnings in the vision.

Many of my Christian friends prayed for my deliverance. But I did not get healed, and the insomnia persisted. I was wondering why my prayers were not being answered. Then, I attended a ministers' conference. After I returned from the conference, I slept well.

The Second Vision

I also saw a second vision. In this one, I saw the same person from the previous vision, but now he was carrying a gun. He was looking for an opportunity to shoot me. I saw myself barely escaping being killed by him. So I stopped communicating with the person from these visions.

THE TEMPTATION OF FAKE LOVE

I began to ponder these matters before the Lord. What is the meaning of all these strange experiences? How did I suddenly get insomnia? As I was praying over it, God also began to impress upon my heart to stay away from a few other individuals whom I *considered* to be friends.

DON'T ACCEPT THEIR LOVE!

After a lengthy season of prayer, I heard the voice of God. God said, "Do not accept their love!" When I heard the voice of God, I was alone in my apartment. Then, I realized that the love and friendship that were given to me by my so-called friends were fake. **The meaning of the two visions that I mentioned is about spiritual contamination, not physical threats. The man that I saw in the visions does not have a violent nature.**

Most people think that the devil will come in with a red suit and a pitchfork in his hand. Don't be naive! The Bible says, "Satan himself is transformed into an angel of light" (2 Corinthians 11:14, KJV). Jesus said that we need to watch out for false prophets who are ferocious wolves; but they will come in sheep's clothing (Matthew 7:15).

CHAPTER TWENTY ONE

THE STRONGHOLD OF

ACCEPTING FAKE LOVE

Albert Speer was the chief architect of Hitler's Nazi Party. After Germany had lost World War II, he was tried and sentenced to 20 years in prison for his involvement in the Nazi party. As "the Nazi who said sorry," he apologized for the great harm that he had caused to others. Speer's brilliant marketing strategy was one of the reasons behind Hitler's political success. Speer promoted an evil monster—Hitler. Sin has the ability to hypnotize us. When we associate with demonized individuals, we will not recognize the danger until it is too late.

In the earlier chapters, I wrote that spiritual warfare happens in the mind of the believer. The devil oppresses a person by building strongholds in his mind. *The area where the stronghold is built becomes the area of demonic activity, and the thought process of the oppressed area comes under the control of the devil.*

THE MIND–THE ENTRY POINT INTO
THE HUMAN SPIRIT

As I discussed in Chapter 9 ("The Battlefield of the Mind"), the word "devil" is the translation of the Greek word *diabolos*. *Diabolos* is a compound of the words *dia* and *ballo* (or *bolos*). The word *dia* means "successfully across." *Ballo* means "to throw, aiming at someone or something." Hence, when the two words *dia* and *ballo* are joined, the meaning is "to throw something until it is fully penetrated." The word *bolos* means "to throw with a casting net."[20] When the two words *dia* and *bolos* are joined, it describes the process of fishing with a net or throwing a net.

In Chapter 10 ("Types of Strongholds"), I wrote about the deliverance of Buddy Harrison. The testimony of Mr. Harrison is a good example of how Satan oppresses Christians by building strongholds. In the life of Harrison, three different strongholds were built by three different demons. Harrison was under the influence of these evil spirits, even though he was a Christian. Through these strongholds, the devil controlled certain areas of his life. These strongholds led to selfishness in three specific areas of his life.

> *15 Then, when desire has conceived, it gives birth to sin; and sin, **when it is full-grown**, brings forth **death**.*
> *16 Do not be deceived, my beloved brethren.*
>
> (James 1:15–16)

In the life of Judas, Satan built a *stronghold of greed*. As a result of this extremely dangerous stronghold, Judas wanted money more than anything. The stronghold of greed turned him into an extremely selfish person. The area of stronghold became the area of selfishness. Sadly, through the stronghold of greed, Satan entered into the spirit of Judas, and Judas became fully demon-possessed. That is the greatest danger of a stronghold. If a Christian is not careful, the devil can enter into his spirit through these strongholds. At this point, that stronghold is full-grown and has brought spiritual death.

THE STRONGHOLD OF ACCEPTING
FAKE LOVE

Judge not according to the appearance, *but judge righteous judgment.*

(John 7:24 KJV)

Strongholds begin with a lie that the devil places in your mind. *So, what is the stronghold of accepting fake love?* The devil is telling you a lie that the **counterfeit** friend loves you. When you are susceptible of establishing friendships without any discernment, you have a **stronghold of accepting fake love**. In some cases, this can be a rational stronghold because the *counterfeit friend* may look exceptionally genuine. The *counterfeit friend* may feel like he is "called" to be your friend. In reality, he is sent by Satan to destroy your life. As you establish friendships with a counterfeit friend, the demons in that person will attach themselves to you. As a result, you become defiled.

I had this particular stronghold; the outward actions of that person I saw in the vision were expressions of love and compassion (See Chapter 20—"Don't Accept Their Love"), but the good character was simply an imitation. My insomnia was the proof of the demonic oppression. I did not know that I was being defiled as I established friendship with that person. I accepted the lie that the person loved me, and as I believed this lie, I became his friend. This *false friendship* gave an open door to the devil to attack me. Through a lack of knowledge in this area, the devil has successfully built the **stronghold of accepting fake love** in the lives of many believers.

THE NET OF FAKE LOVE

The demons resident in the demon-possessed person are carrying a net and throwing the net towards you. **The net is fake love**, and when you accept fake love, you are caught in the net of the devil. You believe the lie that the demon-possessed person loves you, and you become his friend, so the demons in the person will attach themselves to you.

LOVING YOU VS. LOVING THE BENEFITS YOU BRING

If a demon-possessed person is showing great affection to you, it is not because he truly loves you as a person. Instead, the demon-possessed person perceives that you bring great value to him, and he is merely rewarding you for what you are giving him. In other words, the relationship is more like a business transaction. The demon-possessed person may even believe that he loves you, but he is deceived. He does not love you, for a demon-possessed person does not have the capacity to love anyone. Satan is using the body of the demon-possessed person to deceive you through the imitation of love.

THE NET OF REAL LOVE

Jesus told His disciples that He would teach them how to fish for men (Matthew 4:19). A Christian is a fisherman who is carrying the net of the gospel, *the net of real love*. Jesus casts the *net of real love* on us. He wants to bring us into His Kingdom because He loves us. If we do not follow Jesus, we will go to hell.

The devil doesn't do anything original. The early Christian writer, Tertullian, said, "The devil is God's monkey." What Tertullian meant was that the devil's method of operation is that he imitates God. When Satan enters into people, they become demon-possessed and tools of Satan. They may have the appearance of good Christians, but the good character that you see in them is simply an imitation of love. If we foolishly accept their fake love and become their friend, we will fall into deception.

BREAKING THE STRONGHOLD

So here are a few tips on breaking the stronghold of accepting fake love:

1. You need to seek God's guidance before you establish close friendships. Just like Jesus knew the thoughts of others, ask God to reveal the true intentions of your friends.

2. Realize that evil spirits are very real. Demons have possessed many people. On simple observation, it is not possible to know if a person is demon-possessed. As you establish friendships with demon-possessed individuals, you become spiritually contaminated through it.

THE DEVIL'S METHOD

*Put on the whole armor of God, that you may be able to stand against the **wiles** of the devil.*

(Ephesians 6:11)

I want you to pay attention to the phrase, "wiles of the devil." The Greek word for "wiles" is *methodos*, from which we get the English word "method." *Methodos* indicates someone who is on a path to pursue something. The devil has one agenda—to destroy your life. He has a carefully planned strategy to defeat you. He first attacks the mind and in some cases, he even enters the human spirit. If the devil wants to destroy you, he will bring a demon-possessed person into your life. Most likely, the demon-possessed person will have the *appearance* of a true friend. When you establish close fellowship with this person, the evil spirits in that person will attach themselves to you. The devil's method to enter your mind is through the stronghold of accepting fake love.

SPIRITUAL WARFARE IN THE LAST DAYS

*Now as He sat on the Mount of Olives, the disciples came to Him privately, saying, "Tell us, when will these things be? And what will be the sign of Your coming, and of the **end of the age?"***

(Matthew 24:3)

In Matthew 24, the disciples asked Jesus about the sign of His return and of the *end of the age*. The word *age* is translated from the Greek word *aiōn*, which means a period of time.

1 God, who at various times and in various ways spoke in time past to the fathers by the prophets,
*2 has **in these last days spoken to us by His Son**, whom He has appointed heir of all things, through whom also He made the worlds;*

(Hebrews 1:1–2)

A new age began with the birth or ministry of Jesus, and this age is called "the last days" (Hebrews 1:2; Acts 2:16–18). It has lasted about 2,000 years, and we are still living in this period.

*Let no one deceive you by any means; for that Day will not come unless **the falling away** comes first, and **the man of sin is revealed, the son of perdition**,*

(2 Thessalonians 2:3)

The phrase "the son of perdition" refers to the antichrist, who will rule the Earth for seven years. The word "apostasy" comes from the Greek word *apostasia* (translated "falling away" in 2 Thessalonians 2:3). Apostasy means to walk away from the Christian faith or to lose one's salvation. *2 Thessalonians 2:3 says that there will be apostasy ("the falling away") right before the arrival of the antichrist—not as a possibility, but as a certainty.*

*Now the Spirit speaketh expressly, that in **the latter times some shall depart from the faith**, giving heed to seducing spirits, and doctrines of devils;*

(1 Timothy 4:1 KJV)

What does the phrase "latter times" mean? It is a time that is in the future. Now, notice the phrase "depart from the faith." This means that this verse applies to Christians. The apostle Paul is prophesying that seducing spirits will influence some Christians who live in the very last period of time. 2 Thessalonians 2:3 says that there will be apostasy right before the arrival of the antichrist. There will be an increased dimension of spiritual warfare in our days, in comparison to the time of the Early Church because the devil knows that his time is short. In Revelation 12:12, the apostle John saw the increased pressure that the Christians who belong to the *future church* will have to face and said, "For the devil has come down to you, having great wrath, because he knows that he has a short time."

1 Timothy 4:1 says that *seducing spirits* will cause some Christians to fall into apostasy. In Chapter 10 ("Types of Strongholds"), I wrote about how seducing spirits can bombard the mind of people with thoughts of obsession toward someone. However, the workings of seducing spirits cannot be entirely reduced to sexual deviation. Seducing spirits can also cause other types of deception. Seduction is very subtle,

and it is not *open deception*. Seduction means that we cannot find any error based on simple observation, but there are deep dangers that are hidden. *It looks almost right, but it is totally demonic!* It will take the supernatural help of the Holy Spirit to discern the hidden dangers.

DEMON FILLED TIMES?

But know this, that in the last days perilous times will come:
(2 Timothy 3:1)

In 2 Timothy 3:1, Paul is not merely speculating about the condition of the last days. The Greek phrase for "know this" is *touto ginōske,* and it means speaking in full assurance of what will happen. The verb ("will come") is in the future tense. Since the last days began with the birth or ministry of Jesus, 2 Timothy 3:1–5 could apply to Paul's time. While the passage is significant to Paul's time, it has a greater emphasis on what will happen in the future because the verb is used in the future tense. In 2 Timothy 3:1–5, Paul is prophesying of future events, just like he did in 1 Timothy 4:1. The phrase *last days* is repeated in James 5:3.

*Your gold and silver are corroded, and their corrosion will be a witness against you and will eat your flesh like fire. You have heaped up treasure **in the last days**.*
(James 5:3)

*Your gold and silver are corroded. The very wealth you were counting on will eat away your flesh like fire. This corroded treasure you have hoarded will testify against you **on the day of judgment**.*
(James 5:3 NLT)

James 5:3 uses the phrase *the last days* to talk about a future time. The phrase as used in James 5:3 is translated as "the day of judgment" in the New Living Translation. Hence, the implication is at a future time. Thus, the most accurate meaning of the phrase *last days* as used in 2 Timothy 3:1 probably indicates a future time. Paul told Timothy that in the last days perilous times would come. The word translated as **perilous** is the same word that is used to describe the Madman of Gadara (Matthew 8:28), and it is used only twice in the Bible (Matthew 8:28; 2 Timothy 3:1).

> *And when he was come to the other side into the country of the Gergesenes, there met him two possessed with devils, coming out of the tombs, **exceeding fierce**, so that no man might pass by that way.*
>
> (Matthew 8:28 KJV)

The word that is used to describe the Madman of Gadara is *fierce*, which is the same word translated as *perilous* in 2 Timothy 3:1. The Madman of Gadara had thousands of demons in him; he was fully demon possessed! The apostle Paul describes our days as **perilous times**. *Therefore, we can say that we are living in the times of the madman of Gadara—we are living in demon-filled times.* It is the time when demon possession is prevalent. The apostle Paul is giving a prophetic warning of the dangers of our times. Everywhere that you turn, from the tensions in the Middle East to the increasing availability of people to occultic practices, is causing an invasion of the hosts of hell. As we study biblical prophecy, we learn that these things are going to get worse.

THE NET OF FALSE PREACHERS

22 Many will say to Me in that day, 'Lord, Lord, have we not prophesied in Your name, cast out demons in Your name, and done many wonders in Your name?'
23 And then I will declare to them, 'I never knew you; depart from Me, you who practice lawlessness!'

(Matthew 7:22–23)

In some cases, the demon-possessed person can even be a preacher. We need to be very careful of the preachers we allow to influence us. Jesus warns us that Satan's messengers will have the outward appearance of the true servants of God (2 Corinthians 11:13–15). Here are the some of the biblical accounts of *counterfeit* preachers:

1. Jesus and Paul warn about false apostles (Revelation 2:2; 2 Corinthians 11:13).
2. Peter warns about false teachers (2 Peter 2).
3. Jesus, John, and Peter warn about false prophets (Matthew 7:15; Revelation 2:20–22; 1 John 4:1; 2 Peter 2:1–3).
4. Jesus warns about false pastors (John 10:12).

In Matthew 24:4, Jesus said that the *first* sign leading up to His return is deception. In Matthew 24, Jesus warns us four times against deception. Anyone who minimizes the warnings of Jesus is putting himself or herself in great danger. Jesus prophesied that deception would involve three areas:

1. False prophets
2. False messiahs
3. False miracles

When it comes to false prophets in the Pentecostal/charismatic movement, I'd like to point out one issue. Some so-called prophets promise to give prophecies if you pay them a certain amount of money.

In other words, they charge a fixed fee for their prophecies, resembling a visit to a witch doctor or a palm reader. The reason these prophets operate that way is because they have the same evil spirits that witch doctors have. None of the prophets in the Bible charged money to give prophecies. Moreover, how can any prophet promise that he can surely give a prophecy to a certain individual, for God may not have a message for that particular individual?

In one case, a famous prophet who is known for his accurate predictions prophesied to a lady whose husband had cancer. He told her that she had to donate a certain amount (well over $100,000) to "break the curse of cancer" from her husband; this man is a false prophet who prophecies under the influence of evil spirits, yet famous preachers have invited him to preach at their conferences to raise funds for them. *After all, he is smart in raising funds.*

In another case, I once went to the meeting of a well-known Pentecostal prophet who has a worldwide television ministry; some of the most powerful heads of state have invited him to prophesy to them. In the meeting, he said that he wins card games because as a prophet God reveals to him the other person's cards. Another well-known Pentecostal prophet prophecies on his TV program and on his YouTube channel who will win major sports tournaments and even which player will score the goals. I am skeptical of prophecies that predict the winners of sports competitions and of knowing other party's cards in a card game.

There are true prophets in the Pentecostal/charismatic movement. I believe in true prophets, for God can raise a man and empower him with His gifts to be a blessing to millions of people. I know of individuals who stand in the office of the prophet and have large ministries. I pray that God's people will have the discernment to distinguish the true prophets from the false ones.

19 But I trust in the Lord Jesus to send Timothy to you shortly, that I also may be encouraged when I know your state.
20 For I have no one like-minded, who will sincerely care for your state.
*21 **For all seek their own, not the things which are of Christ Jesus**.*
22 But you know his proven character, that as a son with his father he served with me in the gospel.

(Philippians 2:19–22)

The apostle Paul was recommending the ministry of Timothy to the Philippian Church and told about the exceptional character of Timothy. In comparing him to the majority of the preachers of that time, Paul said Timothy was not selfish like the rest. Sadly, here is what Paul said about most of the preachers of the Early Church, "For all seek their own, not the things which are of Christ Jesus."

The Silent Revolution of Deception

*But I fear, lest by any means, as the serpent **beguiled** Eve through his subtlety, so your minds should be **corrupted** from the simplicity that is in Christ.*

(2 Corinthians 11:3 KJV)

This passage was written to the Christians in the Early Church. Paul warned the Christians about the danger of deception. The word "beguile" means to deceive someone, and the Bible repeatedly warns us about deception. First of all, what is deception? Deception is when we believe a lie as the truth. The serpent convinced Eve that God lied to her, but the serpent was lying to Eve. She trusted the serpent more than God—she accepted the *fake love* of the serpent and rejected the true love of God.

In the Garden of Eden, Satan was attacking the mind and emotions of Eve. Eve had no idea that she was being a victim of deception; she believed the lie of the devil and fell into his trap. This is how deception works. Often, when Christians fall into deception, they have no clue that they are being oppressed by the devil. The victims of deception really believe that their thoughts and actions are true; they believe that they are doing the will of God.

> *And that they may recover themselves out of the **snare of**
> **the devil**, who are taken **captive by him at his will**.*
>
> (2 Timothy 2:26 KJV)

The apostle Paul states that a Christian who has become a victim of deception has fallen into the **snare** of Satan. There are degrees of deception, just like there are degrees of demonic bondage. After all, deception is demonic oppression.

Deception can cause our minds to become corrupted just like Eve's mind was corrupted, and we can lose our standing with Christ. Christians can get spiritually contaminated through deception. In some cases, deception can even cause to lose one's salvation. As you can see, this is a very serious matter.

FALSE MENTORS (TOR-MENTORS)

> *Wisdom is better than weapons of war, but **one sinner destroys**
> **much good**.*
>
> (Ecclesiastes 9:18 NIV)

I have been blessed by wonderful godly mentors. I consider them gifts from God. When young people have a desire to know more about God, they go to older successful ministers to learn from their ministerial experiences. This is especially true of young people who are preparing to enter fulltime ministry.

I wanted to learn more about God, and I began to follow certain preachers and their teachings. In my search for genuine ministers, I made the mistake of associating with some people who pretended to be great servants of God. They had selfish agendas and merely used others to get promoted. Eventually, I came to know their true intentions.

You have to be very careful in choosing your mentors. *If you add "tor" before the word "mentor," you get a totally different meaning—tormentor.*

Satan is always looking for access into our lives. One of the fastest ways that Satan gets access into our lives is through wrong relationships; he sends wrong people into our lives in sheep's clothing. Satan does not come as someone who is trying to destroy us—his servants appear to be very loving and caring. If we foolishly welcome everyone who appears to be friendly, we are in great danger. Just like Jesus, we need to know how to discern the true nature of others by listening to their hearts instead of listening to their words or following their actions.

CHAPTER TWENTY TWO

IS LOVE BLIND?

*Wounds from a friend can be trusted, **but an enemy multiplies kisses**.*

(Proverbs 27:6 NIV)

Y ou may deeply love a person and call him or her your best friend. But does that person love you back the same way? Does your friend have the same commitment and affection toward you? I am not saying that your so-called friend is going to betray you—of course, there are extreme cases when betrayals have happened.

I know what it means to go through a *true Judas Iscariot situation*. It is horrible when a betrayal comes from someone you considered to be your closest friends. When we go through heartbreaking experiences of betrayal and disloyalty, we are often tempted to never trust anyone again. It is a wrong approach to close your heart to everyone. The correct approach is to seek God's guidance before you establish close relationships. You need to pray for Divine connections and Divine friendships. There are genuine friends who are waiting for you. You need to ask God to direct you to them.

When a person gets saved, the love of God is poured into his heart (Romans 5:5). When a person becomes born again, his capacity to love expands. Christians make the mistake of viewing the world based on their experiences. It is impossible for non-Christians to deeply love like born-again Christians because the love of God is not poured into their hearts.

Here is another sad reality. There are so many selfish Christians who had a genuine salvation experience, but the strongholds cause them to be selfish in many areas of their lives. However, there is one Person Who loves you deeply—He is Jesus. Let us live for the Person (Jesus) Who loves us the most. Jesus is the best friend you will ever have.

THINK LIKE A SNAKE

*Behold, I am sending you out like sheep in the midst of wolves; **be wary and wise as serpents**, and be innocent (harmless, guileless, and without falsity) as doves.*

(Matthew 10:16 AMP)

Snakes have the ability to camouflage themselves when they enter new territory. Snakes move carefully and do not make any sounds. Jesus is telling us to be as discerning as a snake.

There was a pastor who was faithfully serving the Lord when a lady who was a member of his church asked him to come to her house to pray for her. She said that she was sick and needed prayer for healing, so he innocently went to pray for her. He went alone, and she was alone. After the pastor had left, she called the police and accused him of attempting to rape her. So the pastor was sentenced and put in prison. After a few years, the lady came forward and told the truth. The pastor did not attempt to rape her, and the story was a lie, so the pastor was released from prison.

The pastor truly had an experience like that of Joseph in the Old Testament. Why did this pastor fall into the trap? He accepted the fake love of a demon-possessed lady. *You need to have the ability to discern fake love before it is too late.*

Is Love Blind?

Jesus was not a friend of the religious and secular leaders of his time, but He loved and forgave them as He went to the cross. This should be our example. *Love is not always friendly.* You can love people from a distance and not be their friends. Jesus was not stupid; He saw into the negative realities in a person's life. Love is not stupid. Love sees the negative realities of a person. Growing in discernment does not cause you to become a pessimist; it makes you into a realist.

Sweet Deception

> **Guard your heart above all else**, *for it determines the course of your life.*
>
> (Proverbs 4:23 NLT)

Accepting fake love will give you great joy, but it leads to deception. Sure, the devil will generously pay you, but the cash is counterfeit. There are plenty of demon-possessed people in this world; Satan is in them. The devil is approaching you through these demon-possessed people. The devil, who is resident in them, is carrying a net to trap us. The net is fake love. If a demon-possessed person is showing great affection to you, it is not because he truly loves you as a person. Instead, the demon-possessed person perceives that you bring great value to him, and he is merely rewarding you for what you are giving him. In other words, the relationship is more like a business transaction. The demon-possessed person may even believe that he truly loves you, but he is deceived. He does not love you, for a demon-possessed person does not have the capacity to love anyone.

Fake love is a deadly poison, even though it appears like living water. Many innocent Christians have unknowingly drunk the deadly poison of fake love and became contaminated. The devil will contaminate our lives if we establish friendships with ungodly people. Sometimes, counterfeit friends have sheep's clothing, and they are very convincing.

SPECIAL INSIGHT

*If any of you lacks **wisdom**, let him ask of God, who gives to all liberally and without reproach, and it will be given to him.*

(James 1:5)

The word "wisdom" is translated from the Greek word *sophias*. *Sophias* implies supernatural wisdom or even special insight. W. E. Vines points that *sophias* "is the insight into the true nature of things."[21] It is hard to measure love. Unless we have special insight from God, we cannot look into a person's heart and measure love.

If you are a Christian, you have the Holy Spirit, the true Discerner, dwelling in you. Jesus said that the Holy Spirit will guide us into all truth. Yield your life to Him. As you are filled with the Holy Spirit, and as you walk in obedience to the leading of the Holy Spirit, you will grow into a mature Christian. Spiritual maturity causes you to become a discerning person.

PRAYER FOR DISCERNMENT

I recommend that you pray this prayer for yourself to develop spiritual discernment.

15 Therefore I also, after I heard of your faith in the Lord Jesus and your love for all the saints,

16 do not cease to give thanks for you, making mention of you in my prayers:

17 that the God of our Lord Jesus Christ, the Father of glory, may give to you the spirit of wisdom and revelation in the knowledge of Him,

18 the eyes of your understanding being enlightened; that you may know what is the hope of His calling, what are the riches of the glory of His inheritance in the saints,

19 and what is the exceeding greatness of His power toward us who believe, according to the working of His mighty power

(Ephesians 1:15–19)

14 For this reason I bow my knees to the Father of our Lord Jesus Christ,

15 from whom the whole family in heaven and earth is named,

16 that He would grant you, according to the riches of His glory, to be strengthened with might through His Spirit in the inner man,

17 that Christ may dwell in your hearts through faith; that you, being rooted and grounded in love,

18 may be able to comprehend with all the saints what is the width and length and depth and height —

19 to know the love of Christ which passes knowledge; that you may be filled with all the fullness of God.

20 Now to Him who is able to do exceedingly abundantly above all that we ask or think, according to the power that works in us,

21 to Him be glory in the church by Christ Jesus to all generations, forever and ever. Amen.

(Ephesians 3:14–21)

Prayer of Salvation

Jesus loves you more than any person you have ever met or will meet. You need to recognize the great love that Jesus offers you. If you have never accepted Jesus as your personal Savior, please believe and pray the following:

Dear God in Heaven, I come to you in the Name of Jesus. I acknowledge to You that I am a sinner. Today, I am asking for your forgiveness. Jesus, I believe that You took the punishment of my sins by dying on the cross. Right now, I repent of my sins. I confess Jesus as the Lord of my life. With my heart, I believe that God raised Jesus from the dead. This very moment, I accept Jesus Christ as my own personal Savior, and according to His Word, right now, I am saved.

APPENDIX

Many people use complementary and alternative medicine (CAM) to seek relief from their illnesses. CAM therapies include naturopathy, chiropractic medicine, homeopathic treatment, etc. The National Center for Complementary and Integrative Health is a United States governmental agency which investigates CAM therapies. I have a keen interest in healthcare, and the websites that I often visit to read health-based articles are www.mercola.com, www.doctoroz.com, www.drjaydavidson.com, www.draxe.com, and www.greenmedinfo.com.

Chiropractors are called the drugless doctors. Many professional athletes get regular chiropractic care. Chiropractors focus on the intimate relationship between the nervous system and spine. Chiropractors say that a *misaligned spine* can cause malfunctioning of the nerves, and as a result can cause various illnesses. They believe that fixing the spine will enable the body to heal itself from various diseases.

In Chapter 13 ("Understanding Mental Illness"), I wrote that some chiropractors believe that chiropractic medicine can treat some cases of neuropsychiatric disorders. Chiropractic care may be the answer for some of those who are suffering from neuropsychiatric disorders. The Chiropractic doctor Gerard Martin Pothoff (1889–1937) saw cures of severely mentally ill patients under chiropractic care.[22]

ENDNOTES

1. "What Causes Depression?" Harvard Health Publications, June 9, 2009, accessed September 30, 2015, http://www.health.harvard.edu/mind-and-mood/what-causes-depression.

2. Roxanne Nelson, "Higher Purpose in Life Tied to Better Brain Health," Reuters, Apr 7, 2015, accessed May 2, 2015, http://www.reuters.com/article/us-stroke-risk-attitude-idUSKBN0MY25Q20150407?feedType=RSS&feedName=healthNews.

3. *English Oxford Living Dictionaries*, s.v. "heart," accessed September 22, 2014, http://www.oxforddictionaries.com/us/definition/american_english/heart

4. Gordon Lindsay, ed., *John G. Lake Sermons: Dominion Over Demons, Disease and Death* (1949; repr., Dallas: Christ for the Nations Inc., 2007), 9.

5. Justin Martyr, "Dialogue with Trypho, a Jew," in *The Apostolic Fathers with Justin Martyr and Irenaeus*, ed. Alexander Roberts and James Donaldson, vol. 1, *The Ante-Nicene Fathers* (Grand Rapids: WM. B. Eerdmans, 1979), 240; Irenaeus, "Against Heresies," in *The Apostolic Fathers with Justin Martyr and Irenaeus*, ed. Alexander Roberts and James Donaldson, vol. 1, *The Ante-Nicene Fathers* (Grand Rapids: WM. B. Eerdmans, 1979), 531.

6. Henry George Liddell and Robert Scott, *An Intermediate Greek-English Lexicon: Founded Upon the Seventh Edition of Liddell and Scott's Greek-English Lexicon* (Oxford: Clarendon Press, 1964), 153.

7. Tertullian, *The Writings of Tertullian-Volume 1: On the Spectacles*, in Vol. 11 of *The Ante-Nicene Christian Library*, ed. Rev. Alexander Roberts and James Donaldson (Edinburgh, England: T & T Clark, 1869), 31.

8. Irene Park, *The Witch That Switched* (New Port Richey, Florida: Christ Deliverance Ministries, 1980), 63.

9. Raphael Gasson, *The Challenging Counterfeit* (Plainfield, NJ: Logos

International, 1979), 29.

10. Kenneth E. Hagin, *The Triumphant Church* (Tulsa, OK: Rhema Bible Church, 1993), 76.

11. Ibid., 77–78.

12. H.A. Maxwell Whyte, *Demons and Deliverance* (New Kensington, PA: Whitaker House, 1989), 86–87.

13. Ibid., 87.

14. Joshua Gutierrez, "Many Soldiers Return from War Only to Face Post-Traumatic Stress," Borderzine, April 12,2103, accessed March 25, 2015, http://borderzine. com/2013/04/many-soldiers-a-return-from-war-only-to-face-post-traumatic-stress/.

15. Kenneth E. Hagin, *What to Do When Faith Seems Weak and Victory Lost* (Tulsa, OK: RHEMA Bible Church, 1979), 18–19.

16. Gordon Lindsay, ed., *John G. Lake Sermons: Dominion Over Demons, Disease and Death* (1949; repr., Dallas: Christ for the Nations Inc., 2007), 11.

17. Robert Young, *Analytical Concordance to the Bible*, 20th ed. (New York: Funk & Wagnalls Company, n.d.), viii.

18. Kenneth E. Hagin, *Love: The Way of Victory* (Tulsa: RHEMA Bible Church, 1994), 194–199.

19. Ibid., 199–200.

20. Liddell and Scott, *An Intermediate Greek-English Lexicon*, 153.

21. W. E. Vine, *An Expository Dictionary of New Testament Words: With Their Precise Meanings for English Readers* (Old Tappan: Fleming H. Revell Company, 1966), 4:221.

22. W. Heath Quigley, "Pioneering Mental Health: Institutional Psychiatric Care in Chiropractic," *Chiropractic History* 3, no. 1 (1983): 69–75.

THANKS

Dear Reader,

I hope you enjoyed *Love is Not Blind* and that it has brought great insight into your life. Publishing this book has been very rewarding to me, and I pray that it will be rewarding to you as you put into practice the principles that are expressed in this book.

If you enjoyed the book, I have a kind request: I would very much appreciate a short review on the page where you bought the book to help persuade others to read it. Please join me to spread this message of love and discernment.

Thank you so much for reading *Love is Not Blind*. I truly appreciate it.

In gratitude,
Anuroop Sebastian

ABOUT THE AUTHOR

Anuroop Sebastian is a Bible teacher. Supported by biblical principles, Mr. Sebastian gives his audience a prescription for developing meaningful relationships. Mr. Sebastian completed his Bachelor of Business Administration from the University of Houston. He also graduated in pastoral studies from Christ for the Nations Institute in Dallas, Texas. He resides in Dallas.

www.ingramcontent.com/pod-product-compliance
Lightning Source LLC
Chambersburg PA
CBHW031621040426
42452CB00007B/616